FLOWERS OF HEAVEN

Flowers of Heaven

One Thousand Years of Christian Verse

~

Compiled by
JOSEPH PEARCE

IGNATIUS PRESS   SAN FRANCISCO

Cover art: Lake George, John William Casilear, 1857
© Brooklyn Museum of Art/CORBIS
Cover design by Riz Boncan Marsella

Revised edition © 2005 Ignatius Press, San Francisco
All rights reserved
ISBN 978-1-58617-078-3
ISBN 1-58617-078-3
Library of Congress control number: 2004114949
Printed in the United States of America ∞

For Beatrice

This I implored; and she, so far away,
Smiled, as it seemed, and looked once more at me;
Then unto the eternal fountain turned.

Contents

Acknowledgments

'Twelfth Night' and 'Rose' by Hilaire Belloc are reprinted by permission of The Peters Fraser and Dunlop Group Ltd on behalf of The Estate of Hilaire Belloc; 'Chapel Between Cornfield and Shore' from George Mackay Brown's *Selected Poems* is reprinted by permission of John Murray (Publishers) Ltd; the poetry of Alfred Noyes is reprinted by permission of the Society of Authors as the Literary Representative of the Estate of Alfred Noyes; 'Hill Christmas' and 'Praise' by R. S. Thomas are reprinted by permission of J. M. Dent, a division of the Orion Publishing Group; 'Still Falls the Rain' by Edith Sitwell is reprinted by permission of David Higham Associates Ltd; 'My Body is a Broken Toy' by Maurice Baring is reprinted by permission of A. P. Watt Ltd on behalf of The Trustees of the Maurice Baring Will Trust; Roy Campbell's verse appears by permission of Jonathan Ball Publishers; the poetry of Siegfried Sassoon appears by kind permission of George Sassoon; the poems by Dunstan Thompson are reprinted by permission of Mr Philip Trower, the poet's literary executor. Excerpts from Part II, Part VII and Part X of 'Choruses from "The Rock"' in *Collected Poems 1909–1962* by T. S. Eliot, copyright 1936 by Harcourt, Inc., copyright © 1964, 1963 by T. S. Eliot, reprinted by permission of the publisher.

Finally, I would like to express my gratitude to all those at Ignatius Press who have worked to bring this anthology to fruition.

Preface

The initial motivation for this volume arose from a desire to commemorate the arrival of the third millennium in a way which reflected its overriding Christian significance. It seemed that one way of doing this would be to celebrate the advent of the new millennium with a celebration of the wealth of Christian verse which had been produced during the previous thousand years.

Having decided to undertake the task, it was necessary to set the criteria by which the selection should be made. Above all, the goal was to produce a *balanced* and *representative* cross-section of the finest Christian verse in the English language. The intention has been to produce a selection which is balanced in terms of its chronological distribution throughout the centuries and also in terms of the poets included. Most of the major Christian poets are represented as are most of the major Christian denominations: Catholic, Anglican, Methodist, Puritan, Quaker.

Another conscious decision was to arrange the selection chronologically so that the volume would serve not only as an anthology of verse but also as a history of verse. In order to accentuate the latter aspect, brief biographical and anecdotal introductions have been given to each section. These stress the varied relationships of the poets both with each other and with the trials and tribulations of the often turbulent times in which they lived. These introductions have been kept deliberately short so that they do not interfere with the flow of the verse, but it is hoped that they cement and harmonise the whole, enabling the reader to see the poets and the verse in the historical context in which they belong.

It is also hoped that the right balance has been struck between academic sensibilities and popular taste. Certainly, throughout the preparation of this volume it was always the intention to pass the academic acid test while at the same time retaining the collection's populist appeal. The best of both worlds was the quest and while no anthology can ever please all the people all the time, it is hoped that this selection will at least please most of the people most of the time.

Perhaps, when all else is said and done, the reader alone will make a final judgment regarding the success or otherwise of this volume. It is therefore with an air of trepidation that the following selection is offered. Yet ultimately, of course, the final judgment resides elsewhere and this anthology is intended as a millennial offering in that direction also.

ST HILDEGARD OF BINGEN
(1098–1179)

*The reputation of Hildegard, a Benedictine nun and visionary, has
undergone something of a resurrection in recent years. She was certainly
a woman of many talents, composing hymns, a morality play, commen-
taries on the Gospels, on the Athanasian Creed, and on the Rule of
St Benedict, as well as works of medicine and natural history. She was
a highly gifted artist and her illustrations of her visionary experiences
have been compared with the work of William Blake. Her tremendous
versatility extended to the writing of poetry, two examples of which are
reproduced here.*

The Love of All

Love overflows into all
Glorious from ocean's depths beyond the farthest star,
Bounteous in loving all creation;
For to the King most High
Love has given her kiss of peace.

Mary of Magdala

Holy Mary of Magdala,
you came with a fount of tears
to the Fount of tenderheartedness,
whose glow of overwhelming warmth you felt,
bringing you back from sin to life,
as you found sweet comfort in your bitter pain.
Dear Mary, you have proved yourself
that a sinner may be reconciled to her Creator.
May Christ's loving purpose have mercy on me;
may that same medicine restore my listless soul to health.

You were the Lord's dear love and you knew well that love,
forgiving you your many sins,
because you loved so much!
I am not the worst sinner, blessed Mary,
but I long with hope for that mercy
by which our sins are blotted out.
I am unhappy and plunged into the depths of sin,
weighed down with the burden,
imprisoned in shadows, cut off from myself,
cloaked in darkness.
I have been chosen and loved,
loved by God's own choice,
yet I am unhappy and seek your help, blessed Mary,
for you have made the darkness light.

~

ST FRANCIS OF ASSISI
(1181–1226)

. . . we talk about a man who cannot see the wood for the trees. St Francis was a man who did not want to see the wood for the trees. He wanted to see each tree as a separate and almost a sacred thing, being a child of God and therefore a brother or sister of man.

G. K. Chesterton

Born the son of a wealthy cloth-merchant, St Francis renounced his inheritance and all worldly possessions, choosing a life of voluntary poverty and prayer. For two or three years he lived in solitude as a wandering mendicant. Eventually a small group of disciples gathered round him. This was the birth of the Franciscan order which, along with the Dominicans, was to have a revolutionary and revitalising influence on the life of the Church for centuries afterwards.

'The Canticle of Brother Sun', also known as 'The Lauds of the Creatures', was composed when St Francis was seriously ill at San Damiano, the semi-derelict church that he had rebuilt with his own hands.

∽

The Canticle of Brother Sun

All-highest, almighty good Lord,
to you be praise, glory and honour
and every blessing.
To you alone they are due,
and no man is worthy to speak your name.

Be praised, my Lord, in all your creatures,
especially Brother Sun
who makes daytime,
and through him you give us light.
And he is beautiful, radiant with great splendour,
and he is a sign
that tells, All-highest, of you.

Be praised, my Lord, for Sister Moon and the stars;
you formed them in the sky,
bright and precious and beautiful.

Be praised, my Lord, for Brother Wind,
and for the air and the clouds,
and for fair, and every kind of weather,
by which you give your creatures food.

Be praised, my Lord, for Sister Water,
who is most useful and humble
and lovely and chaste.

Be praised, my Lord, for Brother Fire,
through whom you light up the night for us;
and he is beautiful and jolly
and lusty and strong.

Be praised, my Lord, for our Sister Mother Earth,
who keeps us, and feeds us,
and brings forth fruits of many kinds,
with coloured flowers and plants as well.

Be praised, my Lord, for those who grant pardon
for love of you
and bear with sickness and tribulation.
Blessed are those who bear these things peaceably
because, All-highest,
they will be granted a crown by you.

Be praised, my Lord, for our Sister Bodily Death,
whom no living man can escape.
Woe to those who die in mortal sin!
Blessed are those whom she will find
doing your holy will,
for to them the second death
will do no harm.

Bless and praise my Lord,
thank him, and serve him
in all humility.

Prayer for Peace

Lord. Make me an instrument of your peace.
Where there is hatred let me sow love.
Where there is injury, pardon;
Where there is doubt, faith;
Where there is despair, hope;
Where there is darkness, light;
Where there is sadness, joy.

Divine Master,
Grant that I may seek not so much to be consoled as to console;
To be understood as to understand;
To be loved as to love;
For it is in giving that we receive;
It is in pardoning that we are pardoned,
And it is in dying that we are born to Eternal Life. Amen.

ST GERTRUDE THE GREAT
(*ca.* 1257–1302)

A Benedictine nun and visionary, Gertrude underwent a profound conversion at the age of twenty-five and had various mystical experiences throughout the remaining twenty years of her life. These were based on the Liturgy and many of her visions actually took place during the singing of the Divine Office. She is regarded as one of the most important medieval mystics and was a pioneer of the devotion to the Sacred Heart of Jesus. The first of these verses was composed as a prayer for the Office of Vespers while the second is a prayer on the Te Deum *for the anniversary of a nun's profession.*

Resting in Love

My Love, my God,
you are my dearest possession,
without you I have no hope nor desire
in heaven or in earth.
You are my true inheritance
and all the longing of my life and thought.

My Love,
let the goal of my life
be your pleasure consummated in me!
Show me that covenant of marriage
in which my heart joins with yours.
Show me, as evening draws on,
for you are the light of the evening sky,
the light I see in the face of my dear God.
My Evening Star, dearest and brightest of all,
graciously appear to me at my death,
that I may have the Evening Star of my desire,
and gently fall asleep in all your fullest sweetness,
and find rest in my heart.

Come, fount of eternal light,
take me to yourself from whom I came.
There may I know as I am known,
and love as I am loved,
that I may see you as you are, my God,
and, seeing you, enjoy you and possess you
for evermore.

Love That Nurtures

Holy Trinity,
you are the source
from whom the living Godhead shines, all love and wisdom.
From you springs God's own powerfulness,
insight from your mutual oneness,
overflowing sweetness, love-kindling kindness,
all-embracing holiness, all-pervasive goodness:
yours is the praise, the honour and the glory,
yours is the power and vision of prayer,
yours the offering of thankfulness!

And you, O Love, God yourself,
loving bond of the Holy Trinity,
you lie down to take your rest and pleasure
among earth's children in awesome purity,
yet ablaze with the fire of your love,
like a rose of beauty gathered from among the thorns!

O Love! You only know the paths of truth and living,
in you the Holy Trinity makes covenants of loving,
through you the Spirit's better gifts are working,
from you the seeds that suckle life's fruits are abounding,
from you the sweeter honey of God's joy is flowing,
from you the Lord of hosts pours richer drops of blessing,
the loving promise of the Spirit's treasure,
—rare beyond all measure!

DANTE ALIGHIERI
(1265–1321)

Redeth the grete poete of Ytaille
That highte Dant, for he kan al devyse
Fro point to point; nat o word wol he faille.

Chaucer (from 'The Monk's Tale')

I have just finished an article on Dante . . . and I feel that anything I can say about such a subject is trivial. I feel so completely inferior in his presence—there seems really nothing to do but to point to him and be silent.

T. S. Eliot

'That singular splendour of the Italian race', as Boccaccio dubbed Dante, was born in Florence in May 1265. Baptised Durante, his name was later contracted into Dante and early biographers were eager to stress the aptness of both names, 'the much-enduring' and 'the giver'. Since the time of the Reformation it has been the tendency in England to stress the importance of the Inferno *to the detriment of the other two books of the* Divine Comedy, *with the inevitable result that Dante is perceived by many as dour and puritanical. This does the greatest of poets a great, and dare one say an infernal, injustice. Dante was, above all, a poet of joy as these extracts from Longfellow's translation of* Purgatorio *and* Paradiso *convey.*

O Thou Vain Glory of the Human Powers

In sooth I had not been so courteous
  While I was living, for the great desire
  Of excellence, on which my heart was bent.

Here of such pride is paid the forfeiture;
    And yet I should not be here, were it not
    That, having power to sin, I turned to God.

O thou vain glory of the human powers,
    How little green upon thy summit lingers,
    If't be not followed by an age of grossness!

In painting Cimabue thought that he
    Should hold the field, now Giotto has the cry,
    So that the other's fame is growing dim.

So has one Guido from the other taken
    The glory of our tongue, and he perchance
    Is born, who from the nest shall chase them both.

Naught is this mundane rumour but a breath
    Of wind, that comes now this way and now that,
    And changes name, because it changes side.

What fame shalt thou have more, if old peel off
    From thee thy flesh, than if thou hadst been dead
    Before thou left the *pappo* and the *dindi*,

Ere pass a thousand years? Which is a shorter
    Space to the eterne, than twinkling of an eye
    Unto the circle that in heaven wheels slowest.

With him, who takes so little of the road
    In front of me, all Tuscany resounded;
    And now he scarce is lisped of in Siena,

Where he was lord, what time was overthrown
    The Florentine delirium, that superb
    Was at that day as now 'tis prostitute.

Your reputation is the colour of grass
    Which comes and goes, and that discolours it
    By which it issues green from out the earth.

(*Purgatorio*, Canto XI)

A Warning against Rash Judgements

With this distinction take thou what I said,
   And thus it can consist with thy belief
   Of the first father and of our Delight.

And lead shall this be always to thy feet,
   To make thee, like a weary man, move slowly
   Both to the Yes and No thou seest not;

For very low among the fools is he
   Who affirms without distinction, or denies,
   As well in one as in the other case;

Because it happens that full often bends
   Current opinion in the false direction,
   And then the feelings bind the intellect.

Far more than uselessly he leaves the shore,
   (Since he returneth not the same he went,)
   Who fishes for the truth, and has no skill;

And in the world proofs manifest thereof
   Parmenides, Melissus, Brissus are,
   And many who went on and knew not whither;

Thus did Sabellius, Arius, and those fools
   Who have been even as swords unto the Scriptures
   In rendering distorted their straight faces.

Nor yet shall people be too confident
   In judging, even as he is who doth count
   The corn in field or ever it be ripe.

For I have seen all winter long the thorn
   First show itself intractable and fierce,
   And after bear the rose upon its top;

And I have seen a ship direct and swift
   Run o'er the sea throughout its course entire,
   To perish at the harbour's mouth at last.

Let not Dame Bertha nor Ser Martin think,
   Seeing one steal, another offering make,
   To see them in the arbitrament divine;

For one may rise, and fall the other may.

(Paradiso, Canto XIII)

A Dilemma Concerning Divine Justice

Even as a falcon, issuing from his hood,
   Doth move his head, and with his wings applaud him,
   Showing desire, and making himself fine,

Saw I become that standard, which of lauds
   Was interwoven of the grace divine,
   With such songs as he knows who there rejoices.

Then it began: 'He who a compass turned
   On the world's outer verge, and who within it
   Devised so much occult and manifest,

Could not the impress of his power so make
   On all the universe; as that his Word
   Should not remain in infinite excess.

And this makes certain that the first proud being,
   Who was the paragon of every creature,
   By not awaiting light fell immature.

And hence appears it, that each minor nature
   Is scant receptacle unto that good
   Which has no end, and by itself is measured.

In consequence our vision, which perforce
   Must be some ray of that intelligence
   With which all things whatever are replete,

Cannot in its own nature be so potent,
   That it shall not its origin discern
   Far beyond that which is apparent to it.

Therefore into the justice sempiternal
    The power of vision that your world receives,
    As eye into the ocean, penetrates;

Which, though it see the bottom near the shore,
    Upon the deep perceives it not, and yet
    'Tis there, but it is hidden by the depth.

There is no light but comes from the serene
    That never is o'ercast, nay, it is darkness
    Or shadow of the flesh, or else its poison.

Amply to thee is opened now the cavern
    Which has concealed from thee the living justice
    Of which thou mad'st such frequent questioning.

For saidst thou: "Born a man is on the shore
    Of Indus, and is none who there can speak
    Of Christ, nor who can read, nor who can write;

And all his inclinations and his actions
    Are good, so far as human reason sees,
    Without a sin in life or in discourse;

He dieth unbaptised and without faith;
    Where is this justice that condemneth him?
    Where is his fault, if he do not believe?"

Now who art thou, that on the bench would sit
    In judgment at a thousand miles away,
    With the short vision of a single span?

Truly to him who with me subtilizes,
    If so the Scripture were not over you,
    For doubting there were marvellous occasion.

O animals terrene, O stolid minds,
    The primal will, that in itself is good,
    Ne'er from itself, the Good Supreme, has moved.

So much is just as is accordant with it;
　　No good created draws it to itself,
　　But it, by raying forth, occasions that.'

Even as above her nest goes circling round
　　The stork when she has fed her little ones,
　　And he who has been fed looks up at her,

So lifted I my brows, and even such
　　Became the blessed image, which its wings
　　Was moving, by so many counsels urged.

Circling around it sang, and said: 'As are
　　My notes to thee, who dost not comprehend them,
　　Such is the eternal judgment to you mortals.'

Those lucent splendours of the Holy Spirit
　　Grew quiet then, but still within the standard
　　That made the Romans reverend to the world

It recommenced: 'Unto this kingdom never
　　Ascended one who had not faith in Christ,
　　Before or since he to the tree was nailed.

But look thou, many crying are, "Christ, Christ!"
　　Who at the judgment shall be far less near
　　To him than some shall be who knew not Christ.

Such Christians shall the Ethiop condemn,
　　When the two companies shall be divided,
　　The one for ever rich, the other poor.'

(*Paradiso*, Canto XIX)

～

O Company Elect to the Great Supper

O company elect to the great supper
 Of the Lamb benedight, who feedeth you
 So that for ever full is your desire,

If by the grace of God this man foretaste
 Something of that which falleth from your table,
 Or ever death prescribe to him the time,

Direct your mind to his immense desire,
 And him somewhat bedew; ye drinking are
 For ever at the fount whence comes his thought.

(Paradiso, Canto XXIV)

His Examination in Love

The selfsame voice, that taken had from me
 The terror of the sudden dazzlement,
 To speak still farther put it in my thought;

And said: 'In verity with finer sieve
 Behoveth thee to sift; thee it behoveth
 To say who aimed thy bow at such a target.'

And I: 'By philosophic arguments,
 And by authority that hence descends,
 Such love must needs imprint itself in me;

For Good, so far as good, when comprehended
 Doth straight enkindle love, and so much greater
 As more of goodness in itself it holds;

Then to that Essence (whose is such advantage
 That every good which out of it is found
 Is nothing but a ray of its own light)

More than elsewhither must the mind be moved
 Of every one, in loving, who discerns
 The truth in which this evidence is founded.

Such truth he to my intellect reveals
　　Who demonstrates to me the primal love
　　Of all the sempiternal substances.

The voice reveals it of the truthful Author,
　　Who says to Moses, speaking of Himself,
　　"I will make all my goodness pass before thee."

Thou too revealest it to me, beginning
　　The loud Evangel, that proclaims the secret
　　Of heaven to earth above all other edict.'

And I heard say: 'By human intellect
　　And by authority concordant with it,
　　Of all thy loves reserve for God the highest.

But say again if other cords thou feelest,
　　Draw thee towards Him, that thou mayst proclaim
　　With how many teeth this love is biting thee.'

The holy purpose of the Eagle of Christ
　　Not latent was, nay, rather I perceived
　　Whither he fain would my profession lead.

Therefore I recommenced: 'All of those bites
　　Which have the power to turn the heart of God
　　Unto my charity have been concurrent.

The being of the world, and my own being,
　　The death which He endured that I may live,
　　And that which all the faithful hope, as I do,

With the forementioned vivid consciousness
　　Have drawn me from the sea of love perverse,
　　And of the right have placed me on the shore.

The leaves, wherewith embowered is all the garden
　　Of the Eternal Gardener, do I love
　　As much as he has granted them of good.'

As soon as I had ceased, a song most sweet
    Throughout the heaven resounded, and my Lady
    Said with the others, 'Holy, holy, holy!'

                    (*Paradiso*, Canto XXVI)

O Lady, Thou in Whom My Hope Is Strong

'O Lady, thou in whom my hope is strong,
    And who for my salvation didst endure
    In Hell to leave the imprint of thy feet,

Of whatsoever things I have beheld,
    As coming from thy power and from thy goodness
    I recognise the virtue and the grace.

Thou from a slave hast brought me unto freedom,
    By all those ways, by all the expedients,
    Whereby thou hadst the power of doing it.

Preserve towards me thy magnificence,
    So that this soul of mine, which thou hast healed,
    Pleasing to thee be loosened from the body.'

                    (*Paradiso*, Canto XXXI)

Thou Virgin Mother, Daughter of Thy Son

'Thou Virgin Mother, daughter of thy Son,
    Humble and high beyond all other creature,
    The limit fixed of the eternal counsel,

Thou art the one who such nobility
    To human nature gave, that its Creator
    Did not disdain to make himself its creature.

Within thy womb rekindled was the love,
    By heat of which in the eternal peace
    After such wise this flower has germinated.

Here unto us thou art a noonday torch
  Of charity, and below there among mortals
  Thou art the living fountain-head of hope.

Lady, thou art so great, and so prevailing,
  That he who wishes grace, nor runs to thee,
  His aspirations without wings would fly.

Not only thy benignity gives succour
  To him who asketh it, but oftentimes
  Forerunneth of its own accord the asking.

In thee compassion is, in thee is pity,
  In thee magnificence; in thee unites
  Whate'er of goodness is in any creature.'

(Paradiso, Canto XXXIII)

～

BEFORE CHAUCER

Geoffrey Chaucer is rightly regarded as the father of English poetry but this should not detract from the anonymous poets of the Middle Ages who have bequeathed to us a lasting testament to the rich tradition that existed in Chaucer's time. The following anonymous verses date from the thirteenth, fourteenth and fifteenth centuries.

This World's Joy

Winter wakeneth all my care,
  Now these leaves waxeth bare;
Oft I sigh and mourn sare
  When it cometh in my thought
  Of this world's joy, how it geth all to nought.

Now it is, and now it nys,
  Al so it ner nere, ywys;
That moni mon seith, soth it is:
  All goth bote God's will:
  All we shule deye, thah us like ylle.

Al that gren me graveth grene,
  Now it faleweth al bydene:
Jesu, help that it be seen
  And shield us from hell!
  For y not whider y shal, ne how long here dwell.

A Hymn to the Virgin

Of one that is so fair and bright
   Velut maris stella,
Brighter than the day is light,
   Parens et puella:
I cry to thee, thou see to me,
Lady, pray thy Son for me,
   Tam pia,
That I might come to thee
   Maria.

Al this world was for-lore
   Eva peccatrice,
Till our Lord was y-bore
   De te genetrice.
With *ave* it went away
Thuster nyth and cometh the day
   Salutis;
The well springeth out of thee
   Virtutis.

Lady, flower of all thing,
   Rosa sine spina,
Thou bear Jesu, heaven king,
   Gratia divina:
Of all thou bearst the prize,
Lady, queen of paradise
   Electa:
Maid mild, Mother *es*
   Effecta.

Of a Rose, a Lovely Rose

Listen, lords, both old and young,
How this rose began to spring;
Such a rose to my liking
   In all this world ne know I none.

The angel came from heaven's tower
To greet Mary with great honour,
And said she should bear the flower
   That should break the fiend's bond.

The flower sprung in high Bedlem,
That is both bright and sheen:
The rose is Mary, heaven queen,
   Out of here bosom the blossom sprung.

The first branch is full of might,
That sprung on Christmas night,
The star shone over Bedlem bright
   That is both broad and long.

The second branch sprung to hell,
The fiendish power down to fell:
Therein might none soul dwell;
   Blessed be the time the rose sprung!

The third branch is good and swote,
It sprang to heaven, crop and rote,
Therein to dwell and ben our bote;
   Every day it shows in priest's hand.

Pray we to her with great honour;
She that bear the blessed flower,
She be our help and our succour
   And shields us from the fiend's bond.

Quia Amore Langueo

In the vale of restless mind
  I sought in mountain and in mead,
Trusting a true love for to find,
  Upon an hill then took I heed;
  A voice I heard—and near I yede—
    In huge dolour complaining tho:
  'See, dear soul, my sides bleed,
    Quia amore langueo.'

Under this mount I found a tree;
  Under this tree a man sitting;
From head to foot wounded was he,
  His heart-blood I saw bleeding;
  A seemly man to be a king
    A gracious face to look unto.
  I asked him how he had been paining.
    He said: *Quia amore langueo*.

'I am true love that false was never:
  My sister, man's soul, I loved her thus;
Because I would on no wise dissever,
  I left my kingdom glorious;
  I purveyed her a place full precious;
    She flit, I followed; I loved her so
  That I suffered these pains piteous,
    Quia amore langueo.

'My fair love and my spouse bright,
  I saved her from beating and she hath me bet;
I clothed her in grace and heavenly light,
  This bloody surcote she hath on me set.
  For longing love I will not let;
    Sweet strokes by these, lo!
  I have loved her ever as I het,
    Quia amore langueo.

'I crowned her with bliss, and she me with thorn;
    I led her to chamber, and she me to die;
I brought her to worship, and she me to scorn;
    I did her reverence, and she me villainy.
    To love that loveth is no maistry;
        Her hate made never my love her foe;
    Ask then no mo questions why,
        Quia amore langueo.

'Look unto mine hands, man!
    These gloves were given me when I her sought;
They be not white, but red and wan,
    Embroidered with blood, my spouse them bought;
    They will not off, I leave them nought,
        I woo her with them wherever she go;
    These hands full friendly for her fought,
        Quia amore langueo.

'Marvel not, man, though I sit still;
    My love hath shod me wonder strait;
She buckled my feet, as was her will,
    With sharp nails—well thou maist wait!
    In my love was never deceit,
        For all my members I have opened her to:
    My body I made her heart's bait,
        Quia amore langueo.

'In my side I have made her a nest;
    Look in me how wide a wound is here!
This is her chamber, here shall she rest,
    That she and I may sleep in fere.
    Here may she wash, if any filth were,
        Here is succour for all her woe;
    Come if she will, she shall have cheer,
        Quia amore langueo.

'I will abide till she be ready,
    I will her sue if she say nay;

If she be reckless, I will be ready,
  If she be dangerous, I will her pray.
  If she do weep, then bid I nay;
    Mine arms be spread to clip her me to;
  Cry ones: I come. Now, soul, assay!
    Quia amore langueo.

'I sit on an hill for to see far,
  I look to the vale; my spouse I see:
Now runs she awayward, now comes she nearer,
  Yet from my eye-sight she may not be.
  Some wait their prey to make her flee;
    I run tofore to chastise her foe.
  Recover, my soul, again to me,
    Quia amore langueo.

'My sweet spouse, will we go play?
  Apples be ripe in my garden;
I shall clothe thee in new array,
  Thy meat shall be milk, honey, and wine.
  Now, dear soul, let us go dine,
    Thy sustenance is in my scrippe, lo!
  Tarry not now, fair spouse mine,
    Quia amore langueo.

'If thou be foul, I shall make thee clean;
  If thou be sick, I shall thee heal,
If thou aught mourn, I shall bemene.
  Spouse, why wilt thou nought with me deal?
  Thou foundest never love so leal;
    What wilt thou, soul, that I shall do?
  I may of unkindness thee appeal,
    Quia amore langueo.

'What shall I do now with my spouse?
  Abide I will her gentleness.
Would she look once out of her house
  Of fleshly affections and uncleanness,

Her bed is made, her bolster is bliss,
   Her chamber is chosen, such are no mo.
Look out at the windows of kindness,
   Quia amore langueo.

'Long and love thou never so high,
   Yet is my love more than thine may be;
Thou gladdest, thou weepest, I sit thee by;
   Yet might thou, spouse, look once at me!
   Spouse, should I always feed
      With child's meat? Nay, love, not so!
   I prove thy love with adversity,
      Quia amore langueo.

'My spouse is in chamber, hold your peace;
   Make no noise, but let her sleep.
My babe shall suffer no disease,
   I may not hear my dear child weep;
   For with my pap I shall her keep.
      No wonder though I tend her to:
   This hole in my side had never been so deep,
      But *quia amore langueo.*

'Wax not weary, mine own dear wife:
   What meed is aye to live in comfort?
For in tribulation I run more rife
   Oftentimes than in disport;
   In wealth, in woe, ever I support,
      Then, dear soul, go never me fro!
   Thy meed is marked, when thou art mort,
      Quia amore langueo.'

~

Steadfast Cross

Steadfast cross, among all other
   Thou art a tree of great prize;
In branch and flower such another
   I ne wot non in wood nor rise.
Sweet be the nails, and sweet be the tree,
And sweeter be the burden that hangs upon thee.

Lovely Tear of Lovely Eye

Lovely tear of lovely eye,
   Why dost thou me so wo?
Sorful tear of sorful eye,
   Thou breakst mine heart a-two.

Thou sighest sore,
Thy sorrow is more
   Than man's mouth may tell;
Thou singest of sorrow
Mankind to borrow
   Out of the pit of hell.

I proud and keen,
Thou meek and clean
   Without wo or wile;
Thou art dead for me,
And I live through thee—
   So blissed be that while! . . .

Thine heart is rent,
Thy body is bent
   Upon the rood-tree;
The weather is went,
The devil is shent,
   Christ, through the might of thee.

The Assumption

'Come my sweet, come my flower,
Come my culver, mine own bower,
Come my mother now with me,
For Heaven's queen I make of thee.'

'My sweet Son, with all my love
I come with thee to thine above;
Where thou art now let me be,
For all my love is laid on thee.'

The Rose That Bore Jesu

There is no rose of such virtue
As is the rose that bear Jesu:
　Alleluya!

For in this rose contained was
Heaven and earth in little space,
　Res miranda.

By that rose we may well see
That He is God in persons three,
　Pari forma.

The angels sungen the shepherds to:
'Gloria in excelsis Deo'.
　Gaudeamus!

Leave we all this worldly mirth,
And follow we this joyful birth:
　Transeamus.

By a Chapel

Merry it is in May morning
Merry ways for to gon.

And by a chapel as I come,
Met I with Jesu to churchward gon,
Peter and Paul, Thomas and John,
    And His disciples every one.

Saint Thomas the bells gan ring,
And Saint Collas the mass gan sing;
Saint John took the sweet offering—
    And by a chapel as I com.

Our Lord offered what he would,
A challis all of rich red gold;
Our lady the crown off her molde—
    The son out of her bosom shone.

Saint Jorge that is our Lady's knight,
He tend the tapers fair and bright—
To mine eye a seemly sight—
    And by a chapel as I com.

Prayer for the Journey

Here I am and forth I must,
And in Jesus Christ is all my trust.
No wicked thing do me no dere,
Neither here nor elsewhere.
The Father with me, the Son with me,
The Holy Ghost, and the Trinity,
Be betwixt my ghostly enemy and me.

Corpus Christi Carol

Lully, lulley, lully, lulley;
The falcon hath borne my mate away.

He bare him up, he bare him down,
He bare him into an orchard brown.

In that orchard there was an hall,
That was hanged with purple and pall.

And in that hall there was a bed;
It was hanged with gold so red.

And in that bed there lieth a knight,
His wounds bleeding both day and night.

By that bedside there kneeleth a may,
And she weepeth both night and day.

And by that bedside there standeth a stone,
'Corpus Christi' written thereon.

~

GEOFFREY CHAUCER
(*ca.* 1345–1400)

He is the poet of the dawn, who wrote
    The Canterbury Tales, and his old age
    Made beautiful with song; and as I read
I hear the crowing cock, I hear the note
Of lark and linnet, and from every page
Rise odours of plough'd field or flowery mead.

Henry Wadsworth Longfellow

Chaucer was a poet who came at the end of the medieval age and order . . . the final fruit and inheritor of that order . . . he was much more sane and cheerful and normal than most of the later writers. He was less delirious than Shakespeare, less harsh than Milton, less fanatical than Bunyan, less embittered than Swift.

G. K. Chesterton

Many of the details of Chaucer's life are shrouded in mystery and subject to conjecture but his work stands as a living and permanent monument to his genius.

From *The General Prologue,*
The Canterbury Tales

A good man was ther of religioun,
And was a poure Person of a toun;
But riche he was of hooly thoght and werk.
He was also a lerned man, a clerk,
That Cristes gospel trewely wolde preche.
Hise parisshens devoutly wolde he teche;
Benygne he was, and wonder diligent,
And in adversitee ful pacient,
And swich he was ypreved ofte sithes.
Ful looth were hym to cursen to hise tithes,
But rather wolde he yeven, out of doute,
Unto his poure parisshens aboute
Of his offryng and eek of his substaunce;
He koude in litel thyng have suffisaunce.
Wyd was his parisshe, and houses fer asonder,
But he ne lafte nat, for reyn ne thonder,
In siknesse nor in meschief to visite
The ferreste in his parisshe, muche and lite,
Upon his feet, and in his hand a staf.
This noble ensample to his sheepe he yaf,
That 'first he wroghte and afterward that he taughte'.
Out of the gospel he tho wordes caughte,
And this figure he added eek therto:
That 'if gold ruste, what shal iren doo?'
For if a preest be foul, on whom we truste,
No wonder is a lewed man to ruste;
And shame it is—if a prest take keep—
A filthy shepherde and a clene sheep.
Wel oghte a preest ensample for to yive
By his cleannesse how that his sheep sholde lyve.
He sette nat his benefice to hyre,
And leet his sheepe encombred in the myre
And ran to London, unto Seint Poules,
To seken hym a chaunterie for soules;

Or with a bretherhed to been withholde;
But dwelleth at hoom and kepte wel his folde,
So that the wolf ne made it nat myscarie.
He was a shepherde and noght a mercenarie.
And though he hooly were and vertuous,
He was to synful man nat despitous,
Ne of his speche daungerous ne digne,
But in his techyng discreet and benygne;
To drawen folk to hevene by fairnesse,
By good ensample, this was his bisynesse.
But it were any persone obstinat,
What-so he were, of heigh, or lough estat,
Hym wolde he snybben sharply for the nonys.
A bettre preest I trowe that nowher noon ys.
He waitede after no pompe and reverence,
Ne maked him a spiced conscience;
But Cristes loore and his apostles twelve
He taughte, but first he folwed it hymselve.

From *The Prioress's Tale*

Lady, thy bountee, thy magnificence,
Thy vertu, and thy grete humylitee,
Ther may no tonge expresse in no science;
For somtyme, Lady, er men praye to thee,
Thou goost biforn, of thy benyngnytee,
And getest us the lyght, thurgh thy preyere,
To gyden us unto thy sone so deere.

My konnyng is so wayk, O blisful Queene,
For to declare thy grete worthynesse
That I ne may the weighte nat susteene;
But as a child of twelf monthe oold or lesse,
That kan unnethe any word expresse,
Right so fare I; and therfore I yow preye,
Gydeth my song that I shal of yow seye.

From *The Prioress's Tale*

A litel scole of Cristen folk ther stood
Doun at the ferther ende, in which ther were
Children an heepe, yeomen of Cristen blood,
That lerned in that scole yeer by yere
Swich manere doctrine as men used there;
This is to seyn, to syngen and to rede,
As smale children doon in hire childhede.

Among thise children was a wydwes sone,
A litel clergeon, seven yeer of age,
That day by day to scole was his wone;
And eek also, where-as he saugh thymage
Of Cristes mooder, he hadde in usage,
As hym was taught, to knele adoun and seye
His *Ave Marie*, as he goth by the weye.

Thus hath this wydwe hir litel sone ytaught
Oure blisful Lady, Cristes mooder deere
To worshipe ay; and he forgate it naught,
For sely child wol alday soone leere.
But ay whan I remembre on this mateere,
Seint Nicholas stant evere in my presence,
For he so yong to Crist dide reverence.

This litel child his litel book lernynge,
As he sat in the scole at his prymer,
He *Alma Redemptoris* herde synge,
As children lerned hire antiphoner.
And as he dorste, he droug hym ner and ner,
And herkned ay the wordes and the noote,
Til he the firste vers koude al by rote.

Noght wiste he what this Latyn was to seye,
For he so yong and tendre was of age;
But on a day his felawe gan he preye
Texpounden hym this song in his language

Or telle hym why this song was in usage.
This preyde he hym to construe and declare
Ful often tyme upon hise knowes bare.

His felawe, which that elder was than he,
Answerde hym thus: 'This song, I have herd seye,
Was maked of our blisful Lady free,
Hire to salue, and eek hire for to preye
To been oure help and socour whan we deye.
I kan namoore expounde in this mateere;
I lerne song, I kan but smal grammeere.'

'And is this song maked in reverence
Of Cristes mooder?' seyde this innocent.
'Now certes I wol do my diligence
To konne it al er Cristemasse is went;
Though that I for my prymer shal be shent,
And shal be beten thries in an houre,
I wol it konne Oure Lady for to honoure.'

His felawe taughte hym homward prively,
Fro day to day, til he koude it by rote;
And thanne he song it wel and boldely
Fro word to word, acordynge with the note.
Twies a day it passed thurgh his throte,
To scole ward and homward whan he wente
On Cristes mooder set was his entente.

JOHN LYDGATE
(*ca.* 1370–1450)

The poetry of John Lydgate owes much to the influence of Chaucer.
Born near Newmarket, Lydgate became a Benedictine monk at Bury
St Edmunds and travelled in France and possibly Italy before becoming
Prior of Hatfield Broadoak in 1423. A court poet, he received a pension
in 1439, but died in poverty.

Vox Ultima Crucis

Tarry no longer; toward thine heritage
Hast on thy way, and be of right good cheer.
Go each day onward on thy pilgrimage;
Think how short time thou hast abiden here.
Thy place is bygged above the stars clear,
Noon earthly palace wrought in so stately wise.
Come on, my friend, my brother most entere!
For thee I offered my blood in sacrifice.

~

JOHN WALTON
(*fl. ca.* 1410)

God, the Port of Peace

Now cometh all ye that been y-brought
  In bonds full of busy bitterness,
Of earthly lusts abiding in your thought!
  Here is the rest from all your business,
  Here is the port of peace and restfulness
    To them that stand in storms and disease,
  Refuge overt to wretches in distress,
    And all comfort from mischief and misease.

~

WILLIAM DUNBAR
(*ca.* 1465–1520)

As a poet, Dunbar has been described as 'at times as rich in fancy and colour as Spenser in the Faerie Queen; *as homely and shrewd and coarse as Chaucer in the* Miller's Tale; *as pious and devotional as Cowper in his hymns; and as wildly grotesque in satire as Burns'.*

On the Nativity of Christ

Rorate coeli desuper!
  Heavens, distil your balmy showers!
For now is risen the bright day-star,
  From the rose Mary, flower of flowers:
  The clear Son, whom no cloud devours,
Surmounting Phoebus in the East,
  Is coming off his heavenly towers:
    Et nobis Puer natus est.

Archangels, angels, and dominations,
  Thrones, powers, and martyrs seir,
And all ye heavenly operations,
  Star, planet, firmament, and sphere,
  Fire, earth, air, and water clear,
To Him give loving, most and lest,
  That come in so meek manner;
    Et nobis Puer natus est.

Sinners be glad, and penance do,
  And thank your Maker heartfully;
For he that ye might not come to
  To you is coming full humbly
  Your souls with his blood to buy
And loose you of the fiend's arrest—
  And only of his own mercy;
    Pro nobis Puer natus est.

All clergy do to him incline,
　And bow unto that bairn benign,
And do your observance divine
　　To him that is of kings King:
　　Incense his altar, read and sing
In holy kirk, with mind digest,
　Him honouring attower all thing
　　Qui nobis Puer natus est.

Celestial fowls in the air,
　Sing with your notes upon the height,
In firths and in forests fair
　　Be mirthful now at all your might;
　　For passed is your dully night,
Aurora has the clouds pierced,
　The Son is risen with gladsome light,
　　Et nobis Puer natus est.

Now spring up flowers from the root,
　Revert you upward naturally,
In honour of the blessed fruit
　　That rose up from the rose Mary;
　　Lay out your leaves lustily,
From death take life now at the lest
　In worship of that Prince worthy
　　Qui nobis Puer natus est.

Sing, heaven imperial, most of height!
　Regions of air make harmony!
All fish in flood and fowl of flight
　　Be mirthful and make melody!
　　All *Gloria in excelsis* cry!
Heaven, earth, sea, man, bird, and beast,
　He that is crowned above the sky
　　Pro nobis Puer natus est!

BEFORE THE STORM

As the fifteenth century drew to a close none could have known that within fifty years the Church in England would be torn asunder in the rupture of the Reformation. These two anonymous poems, written in this period, are evocative of the Christian calm before the storm.

Carol

I sing of a maiden
   That is matchless;
King of all kings
   To her son she ches.

He came all so still
   There his mother was,
As dew in April
   That falleth on the grass.

He came all so still
   To his mother's bower,
As dew in April
   That falleth on the flower.

He came all so still
   There his mother lay,
As dew in April
   That falleth on the spray.

Mother and maiden
   Was never none but she;
Well may such a lady
   God's mother be.

Cradle Song

O my dear heart, young Jesus sweet,
Prepare thy cradle in my spreet,
And I shall rock thee in my heart
And never more from thee depart.

But I shall praise thee evermoir
With songs sweet unto thy gloir;
The knees of my heart shall I bow,
And sing that right *Balulalow!*

THE STORM

In the wrackes of Walsingham
    Whom should I choose
But the Queen of Walsingham
    To be guide to my muse.

St Philip Howard, Earl of Arundel
(From 'The Lament for Walsingham')

Perhaps the best way to evoke in verse the rupture of the Church in England is through the medium of two sixteenth-century poems relating to Walsingham. By the beginning of the sixteenth century the shrine at Walsingham had been a place of pilgrimage for more than 450 years and had become the principal Marian shrine of the whole of Christendom. A succession of English monarchs had made pilgrimages there and pilgrims arrived from all over Europe. In 1538 the shrine was destroyed. The first of these two poems, attributed to Sir Walter Raleigh, harks back to the years before the shrine's destruction, the second, attributed to the English Martyr, St Philip Howard, laments its loss. Although the first is not, strictly speaking, an overtly Christian verse, its comparison of true love with the follies of worldly love is poignant in relation to Henry VIII's relationship with the Church and with his wives.

As Ye Came from the Holy Land

As ye came from the holy land
  Of Walsinghame,
Met you not with my true love
  By the way as you came?

How should I know your true love,
  That have met many a one
As I came from the holy land,
  That have come, that have gone?

She is neither white nor brown,
  But as the heavens fair;
There is none hath her form divine
  In the earth or the air.

Such a one did I meet, good sir,
  Such an angelic face,
Who like a nymph, like a queen, did appear
  In her gait, in her grace.

She hath left me here alone
  All alone, as unknown,
Who sometime did me lead with herself,
  And me loved as her own.

What's the cause that she leaves you alone
  And a new way doth take,
That sometime did love you as her own,
  And her joy did you make?

I have loved her all my youth,
  But now am old, as you see:
Love likes not the falling fruit,
  Nor the withered tree.

Know that Love is a careless child,
  And forgets promise past:

He is blind, he is deaf when he list,
    And in faith never fast.

His desire is a dureless content,
    And a trustless joy;
He is won with a world of despair,
    And is lost with a toy.

Of womenkind such indeed is the love,
    Or the word love abused,
Under which many childish desires
    And conceits are excused.

But true love is a durable fire,
    In the mind ever burning,
Never sick, never dead, never cold,
    From itself never turning.

The Lament for Walsingham

Bitter, bitter oh to behold
The grass to grow
Where the walls of Walsingham
So stately did show.

Such were the worth of Walsingham
While she did stand,
Such are the wrackes as now do show
Of that so holy land.

Level, level with the ground
The Towers do lie
Which with their golden, glitt'ring tops
Pierced out to the sky.

Where were gates no gates are now,
The ways unknown,
Where the press of friars did pass
While far her fame was blown.

Owls do scrike where the sweetest hymns
Lately were sung,
Toads and serpents hold their dens
Where the palmers did throng.

Weep, weep, O Walsingham,
Whose days are nights,
Blessings turned to blasphemies,
Holy deeds to dispites.

Sin is where our Lady sat,
Heaven turned to hell;
Satan sits where our Lord did sway,
Walsingham, oh, farewell!

~

ST ROBERT SOUTHWELL
(1561–1595)

Robert Southwell was born in the very midst of the storm which beset the Christian Church in England during the sixteenth century. His father, though initially a recusant, eventually conformed to the practices of the recently founded Anglican Church. Southwell, however, found it impossible in conscience to follow his father. He went into exile where he studied in Douai, Paris and Rome before returning to England as a Jesuit priest in 1586. He was arrested in 1592 and imprisoned in the Tower and at Newgate. After three years of incarceration, during which time he was tortured repeatedly, he was tried and condemned as a priest. He was hanged, drawn and quartered at Tyburn on 21 February 1595. In 1970 he was canonised by Pope Paul VI as one of the Forty Martyrs of England and Wales. Robert Southwell was only thirty-three at the time of his execution but in his short and dramatic life he wrote some of the finest religious poetry in the English language.

Marie Magdalen's Complaint at Christ's Death

Since my life from life is parted:
   Death come take thy portion,
Who survives, when life is murdered,
   Lives by mere extortion.
All that live, and not in God,
Couch their life in death's abode.

Silly stars must needs leave shining,
   When the sun is shadowed.
Borrowed streams refrain their running,
   When head springs are hindered.
One that lives by other's breath,
Dieth also by his death.

O true life, since thou hast left me,
   Mortal life is tedious,
Death it is to live without thee,
   Death of all most odious.
Turn again, or take me to thee,
Let me die or live thou in me.

Where the truth once was and is not,
   Shadows are but vanity:
Shewing want, that help they cannot,
   Signs, not salves of misery.
Painted meat no hunger feeds,
Dying life each death exceeds.

With my love, my life was nestled
   In the sum of happiness;
From my love, my life is wrested
   To a world of heaviness.
O, let love my life remove,
Since I live not where I love.

O my soul what did unloose thee
   From the sweet captivity?

God, not I, did still possess thee:
   His, not mine thy liberty.
O, too happy thrall thou wert,
When thy prison was his heart.

Spiteful spear, that break'st this prison,
   Seat of all felicity,
Working this, with double treason,
   Love's and life's delivery:
Though my life thou drav'st away,
Maugre thee my love shall stay.

The Burning Babe

As I in hoary winter's night
   Stood shivering in the snow,
Surprised I was with sudden heat,
   Which made my heart to glow;

And lifting up a fearful eye,
   To view what fire was near,
A pretty Babe all burning bright
   Did in the air appear;

Who, scorched with excessive heat,
   Such floods of tears did shed,
As though his floods should quench his flames
   Which with his tears were fed:

'Alas', quoth he, 'but newly born,
   In fiery heats I fry,
Yet none approach to warm their hearts
   Or feel my fire, but I.

'My faultless breast the furnace is,
   The fuel wounding thorns:
Love is the fire, and sighs the smoke,
   The ashes, shames and scorns;

The fuel Justice layeth on,
     And Mercy blows the coals,
The metal in this furnace wrought
     Are mens defiled souls:

'For which, as now on fire I am
     To work them to their good,
So will I melt into a bath
     To wash them in my blood.'

With this he vanished out of sight
     And swiftly shrunk away,
And straight I called unto mind
     That it was Christmas day.

New Heaven, New War

Come to your heaven you heavenly choirs,
Earth hath the heaven of your desires;
Remove your dwelling to your God,
A stall is now his best abode;
Since men their homage do deny,
Come Angels all their fault supply.

His chilling cold doth heat require,
Come Seraphims in lieu of fire;
This little Ark no cover hath,
Let Cherubs wings his body swath:
Come Raphael, this Babe must eat,
Provide our little Tobie meat.

Let Gabriel be now his groom,
That first took up his earthly room;
Let Michael stand in his defence,
Whom love hath linked to feeble sense,
Let Graces rock when he doth cry,
Let Angels sing his lullaby.

The same you saw in heavenly seat,
Is he that now sucks Mary's teat;
Agnize your King a mortal wight,
His borrowed weed lets not your sight;
Come kiss the manger where he lies,
That is your bliss above the skies.

This little Babe so few days old,
Is come to rifle Satan's fold;
All hell doth at his presence quake,
Though he himself for cold does shake:
For in this weak unarmed wise,
The gates of hell he will surprise.

With tears he fights and wins the field,
His naked breast stands for a shield;
His battering shot are babish cries,
His Arrows looks of weeping eyes,
His Martial ensigns cold and need,
And feeble flesh his warrior's steed.

His Camp is pitched in a stall,
His bulwark but a broken wall:
The Crib his trench, hay stalks his stakes,
Of shepherds he his Muster makes;
And thus as sure his foe to wound,
The Angels trumps alarum sound.

My soul with Christ join thou in fight,
Stick to the tents that he hath dight;
Within his Crib is surest ward,
This little Babe will be thy guard:
If thou wilt foil thy foes with joy,
Then flit not from the heavenly boy.

New Prince, New Pomp

Behold, a silly tender Babe
  In freezing winter night
In homely manger trembling lies,
  Alas, a piteous sight!

The inns are full; no man will yield
  This little pilgrim bed,
But forced he is with silly beasts
  In crib to shroud his head.

Despise him not for lying there.
  First, what he is inquire;
An orient pearl is often found
  In depth of dirty mire.

Weigh not his crib, his wooden dish,
  Nor beasts that by him feed;
Weigh not his Mother's poor attire,
  Nor Joseph's simple weed.

This stable is a Prince's court,
  This crib his chair of state;
The beasts are parcel of his pomp,
  The wooden dish his plate.

The persons in that poor attire
  His royal liveries wear;
The Prince himself is come from heaven;
  This pomp is prized there.

With joy approach, O Christian wight,
  Do homage to thy King;
And highly prize his humble pomp,
  Which he from heaven doth bring.

Content and Rich

I dwell in Grace's court,
   Enriched with Virtue's rights;
Faith guides my wit, Love leads my will,
   Hope all my mind delights.

In lowly vales I mount
   To pleasure's highest pitch;
My silly shroud true honour brings;
   My poor estate is rich.

My conscience is my crown,
   Contented thoughts my rest;
My heart is happy in itself
   My bliss is in my breast.

Enough, I reckon wealth;
   A mean the surest lot,
That lies too high for base contempt,
   Too low for envy's shot.

My wishes are but few,
   All easy to fulfil;
I make the limits of my power
   The bonds unto my will.

I have no hopes but one,
   Which is of heavenly reign;
Effects attained, or not desired,
   All lower hopes refrain.

I feel no care of coin;
   Well-doing is my wealth;
My mind to me an empire is,
   While grace affordeth health.

I clip high-climbing thoughts,
   The wings of swelling pride;
Their fall is worst, that from the height
   Of greatest honour slide.

Sith sails of largest size
    The storm doth soonest tear,
I bear so low and small a sail
    As freeth me from fear.

I wrestle not with rage,
    While fury's flame doth burn;
It is in vain to stop the stream
    Until the tide doth turn.

But when the flame is out,
    And ebbing wrath doth end,
I turn a late enraged foe
    Into a quiet friend.

And taught with often proof,
    A tempered calm I find
To be most solace to itself,
    Best cure for angry mind.

Spare diet is my fare,
    My clothes more fit than fine;
I know I feed and clothe a foe
    That pampered would repine.

I envy not their hap,
    Whom favour doth advance;
I take no pleasure in their pain,
    That have less happy chance.

To rise by other's fall
    I deem a losing gain:
All states with others' ruin built
    To ruin run amain.

No change of Fortune's calms
    Can cast my comforts down;
When Fortune smiles, I smile to think
    How quickly she will frown.

And when in froward mood
　　She proves an angry foe,
　Small gain I found to let her come,
　　Less loss to let her go.

From *Of the Blessed Sacrament of the Altar*

The angels' eyes, whom veils cannot deceive,
　Might best disclose that best they do discern;
Men must with sound and silent faith receive
　More than they can by sense or reason learn;
God's power our proofs, His works our wit exceed,
The doer's might is reason of His deed.

A body is endued with ghostly rights;
　And Nature's work from Nature's law is free;
In heavenly sun lie hid eternal lights,
　Lights clear and near, yet them no eye can see;
Dead forms a never-dying life do shroud;
A boundless sea lies in a little cloud.

The God of Hosts in slender host doth dwell,
　Yea, God and man with all to either due,
That God that rules the heavens and rifled hell,
　That man whose death did us to life renew:
That God and man that is the angels' bliss,
In form of bread and wine our nurture is.

Whole may His body be in smallest bread,
　Whole in the whole, yea whole in every crumb;
With which be one or be ten thousand fed,
　All to each one, to all but one doth come;
And though each one as much as all receive,
Not one too much, nor all too little have.

One soul in man is all in every part;
　One face at once in many mirrors shines;

One fearful noise doth make a thousand start;
   One eye at once of countless things defines;
If proofs of one in many Nature frame,
God may in stranger sort perform the same.

God present is at once in every place,
   Yet God in every place is ever one;
So may there be by gifts of ghostly grace,
   One man in many rooms, yet filling none;
Since angels may effects of bodies shew,
God angels' gifts on bodies may bestow.

What God as author made he alter may,
   No change so hard as making all of naught;
If Adam framed was of slimy clay,
   Bread may to Christ's most sacred flesh be wrought.
He may do this that made with mighty hand
Of water wine, a snake of Moses' wand.

Seek Flowers of Heaven

Soar up my soul unto thy rest,
   Cast off this loathsome load;
Long is the date of thy exile,
   Too long thy strait abode.

Graze not on worldly withered weed,
   It fitteth not thy taste,
The flowers of everlasting spring
   Do grow for thy repast.

Their leaves are stained in beauty's dye,
   And blazed with their beams,
Their stalks enameled with delight,
   And limbed with glorious gleams.

Life giving juice of living love
   Their sugared veins doth fill,
And watered with eternal showers,
   They nectared drops distill.

These flowers do spring from fertile soil,
    Though from unmanured field,
Most glittering gold in lieu of glebe
    These fragrant flowers doth yield;

Whose sovereign scent surpassing sense
    So ravisheth the mind,
That worldly weeds needs must he loathe,
    That can these flowers find.

Upon the Image of Death

Before my face the picture hangs,
    That daily should put me in mind
Of those cold qualms, and bitter pangs,
    That shortly I am like to find;
But yet alas full little I
    Do think hereon that I must die.

I often look upon a face
    Most ugly, grisly, bare, and thin,
I often view the hollow place,
    Where eyes, and nose, had sometimes been,
I see the bones across that lie;
    Yet little think that I must die.

I read the label underneath
    That telleth me whereto I must,
I see the sentence eake that saith,
    Remember man that thou art dust;
But yet alas but seldom I
    Do think indeed that I must die.

Continually at my bed's head,
    A hearse doth hang which doth me tell,
That I yer morning may be dead,
    Though now I feel my self full well;
But yet alas, for all this I
    Have little mind that I must die.

The gown which I do use to wear,
    The knife wherewith I cut my meat,
And eke that old and ancient chair,
    Which is my only usual seat;
All those do tell me I must die,
    And yet my life amend not I.

My ancestors are turned to clay,
    And many of my mates are gone,
My youngers daily drop away,
    And can I think to scape alone?
No, no, I know that I must die,
    And yet my life amend not I.

Not Solomon for all his wit,
    Nor Samson though he were so strong,
No king nor person ever yet
    Could scape, but death laid him along;
Wherefore I know that I must die,
    And yet my life amend not I.

Though all the East did quake to hear,
    Of Alexander's dreadful name,
And all the West did likewise fear,
    To hear of Julius Caesar's fame,
Yet both by death in dust now lie,
    Who then can scape but he must die?

If none can scape death's dreadful dart,
    If rich and poor his beck obey,
If strong, if wise, if all do smart,
    Then I to scape shall have no way.
Oh grant me grace O God that I,
    My life may mend since I must die.

The Assumption of Our Lady

If sin be captive grace must find release,
From curse of sin the innocent is free,
Tomb prison is for sinners that decease,
No tomb but throne to guiltless doth agree.
Though thralls of sin lie lingering in their grave
Yet faultless corpse with soul reward must have.

The dazzled eye doth dimmed light require
And dying sights repose in shrouding shades,
But Eagles' eyes to brightest light aspire
And living looks delight in lofty glades.
Faint winged fowl by ground doth faintly fly,
Our Princely Eagle mounts unto the sky.

Gem to her worth, spouse to her love ascends,
Prince to her throne, Queen to her heavenly king,
Whose court with solemn pomp on her attends,
And Quires of Saints with greeting notes do sing.
Earth rendereth up her undeserved prey,
Heaven claims the right and bears the prize away.

A Child My Choice

Let folly praise that fancy loves, I praise and love that Child
Whose heart no thought, whose tongue no word, whose hand
no deed defiled.
I praise him most, I love him best, all praise and love is his,
While him I love, in him I live, and cannot live amiss.
Love's sweetest mark, laud's highest theme, man's most desired
light,
To love him life, to leave him death, to live in him delight.
He mine by gift, I his by debt, thus each to other due,
First friend he was, best friend he is, all times will try him true.

Though young, yet wise; though small, yet strong; though man,
yet God he is:

As wise he knows; as strong he can; as God he loves to bliss.
His knowledge rules; his strength defends; his love doth cherish
    all;
His birth our Joy; his life our light; his death our end of thrall.
Alas, he weeps, he sighs, he pants, yet do his Angels sing;
Out of his tears, his sighs and throbs, doth bud a joyful spring.
Almighty babe, whose tender arms can force all foes to fly,
Correct my faults, protect my life, direct me when I die.

~

SIR WALTER RALEIGH
(1552–1618)

Sir Walter Raleigh, like St Robert Southwell, was a victim of the volatile politics of the sixteenth and seventeenth centuries, suffering both prolonged imprisonment and finally execution in the reign of James I. In the reign of Elizabeth, however, he had been a favourite of the Queen and had prospered greatly as a result. Perhaps he is best known to posterity as a courtier, navigator and adventurer, being remembered as the person responsible for introducing potatoes and tobacco into England. Yet he was also a poet of great note. His greatest achievement in verse was 'The Passionate Man's Pilgrimage', allegedly written on the night before he was beheaded. In fact, it was probably written fifteen years earlier when he was initially sentenced to death in November 1603. This, however, detracts nothing from the poem's power because it is likely that when it was written Raleigh genuinely believed he would be executed the following morning. Only on the scaffold itself was the sentence of death commuted to perpetual imprisonment.

The Passionate Man's Pilgrimage

Give me my Scallop shell of quiet,
My staff of Faith to walk upon,
My Scrip of Joy, Immortal diet,
My bottle of salvation:
My Gown of Glory, hope's true gauge,
And thus I'll take my pilgrimage.

Blood must be my body's balmer,
No other balm will there be given
Whilst my soul like a white Palmer
Travels to the land of heaven,
Over the silver mountains,
Where spring the Nectar fountains:

And there I'll kiss
The bowl of bliss,
And drink my eternal fill
On every milky hill.
My soul will be adry before,
But after it will thirst no more.

And by the happy blissful way
More peaceful Pilgrims I shall see,
That have shaken off their gowns of clay,
And go appareled fresh like me.
I'll bring them first
To slake their thirst
And then to taste those Nectar suckets
At the clear wells
Where sweetness dwells,
Drawn up by Saints in Crystal buckets.

And when our bottles and all we,
Are filled with immortality:
Then the holy paths we'll travel
Strewed with Rubies thick as gravel,
Ceilings of diamonds, sapphire floors,
High walls of coral and pearl bowers.
From thence to Heaven's bribeless hall
Where no Corrupted Lawyers brawl
No Conscience molten into gold,
Nor forged accusers bought and sold,
No cause deferred, nor vain spent Journey,
For there Christ is the King's Attorney:
Who pleads for all without degrees,
And he hath Angels, but no fees.

When the grand twelve million Jury
Of our sins with dreadful fury,
Gainst our souls black verdicts give,
Christ pleads his death, and then we live,
Be thou my speaker, taintless pleader,

Unblotted Lawyer, true proceeder,
Thou movest salvation even for alms:
Not with a bribed Lawyer's palms.

And this is my eternal plea,
To him that made Heaven, Earth and Sea,
Seeing my flesh must die so soon,
And want a head to dine next noon,
Just at the stroke when my veins start and spread
Set on my soul an everlasting head.
Then am I ready like a palmer fit,
To tread those blest paths which before I writ.

What Is Our Life?

What is our life? A play of passion,
Our mirth the music of division,
Our mothers' wombs the trying houses be,
Where we are dressed for this short Comedy,
Heaven the Judicious sharp spectator is,
That sits and marks still who doth act amiss,
Our graves that hide us from the searching Sun,
Are like drawn curtains when the play is done,
Thus march we playing to our latest rest,
Only we die in earnest, that's no Jest.

The Conclusion

Even such is Time, that takes in trust
Our youth, our joys, our all we have,
And pays us but with earth and dust;
     Who in the dark and silent grave,
When we have wandered all our ways,
Shuts up the story of our days;
But from this earth, this grave, this dust,
My God shall raise me up, I trust.

THOMAS GOODING
(16th Century)

The following epitaph, carved into the wall of Norwich Cathedral, dates from the sixteenth century. Whether written by Thomas Gooding before his death, or by an acquaintance after it, the short verse serves as a timely reminder of the egalitarianism of mortality.

Epitaph

All you that do this place pass bye
Remember death for you must dye.
As you are now even so was I
And as I am so shall you be.
Thomas Gooding here do staye
Waiting for God's judgement daye.

∼

ANONYMOUS
(16th Century)

If the sombre words on Thomas Gooding's tomb serve as a reminder of death, the words of this anonymous sixteenth-century verse express the Christian hope of the life that follows it.

Hierusalem

Hierusalem, my happy home,
    When shall I come to thee?
When shall my sorrows have an end,
    Thy joys when shall I see?

O happy harbour of the saints,
    O sweet and pleasant soil,
In thee no sorrow may be found,
    No grief, no care, no toil.

There lust and lucre cannot dwell,
    There envy bears no sway;
There is no hunger, heat, nor cold,
    But pleasure every way.

Thy walls are made of precious stones,
    Thy bulwarks diamonds square;
Thy gates are of right orient pearl,
    Exceeding rich and rare.

Thy turrets and thy pinnacles
    With carbuncles do shine;
Thy very streets are paved with gold,
    Surpassing clear and fine.

Ah, my sweet home, Hierusalem,
    Would God I were in thee!

Would God my woes were at an end,
    Thy joys that I might see!

Thy gardens and thy gallant walks
    Continually are green;
There grows such sweet and pleasant flowers
    As nowhere else are seen.

Quite through the streets, with silver sound,
    The flood of life doth flow;
Upon whose banks on every side
    The wood of life doth grow.

There trees for evermore bear fruit,
    And evermore do spring;
There evermore the angels sit,
    And evermore do sing.

Our Lady sings *Magnificat*
    With tune surpassing sweet;
And all the virgins bear their part,
    Sitting about her feet.

Hierusalem, my happy home,
    Would God I were in thee!
Would God my woes were at an end,
    Thy joys that I might see!

~

ALEXANDER MONTGOMERIE
(*ca.* 1545–*ca.* 1610)

Montgomerie was 'maister poet' to James VI of Scotland but was denounced as a rebel in 1597 after being implicated in Barclay of Ladyland's Catholic plot.

Away Vain World

Away vain world, bewitcher of my heart!
My sorrow shows, my sin makes me to smart!
  Yet will I not despair
  But to my God repair—
    He has mercy ay,
    Therefore will I pray.
He has mercy ay and loves me
Though by his humbling hand he proves me.

Away, away, too long thou has me snared!
I will not tyne more time, I am prepared
  Thy subtle sleights to fly,
  Which have allured me.
    Though they sweetly smile,
    Smoothly they beguile:
Though they sweetly smile, I fear them.
I find them false, I will forebear them.

Once more away, shows loth the world to leave,
Bids oft adieu with it that holds me slave.
  Loth am I to forgo
  This sweet alluring foe.
    Since thy ways are vain,
    Shall I thee retain?
Since thy ways are vain, I quite thee.
Thy pleasures shall no more delight me.

A thousand times away! Oh, say no more!
Sweet Christ conduct, lest subtle sin devour!
  Without thy helping hand
  No man has strength to stand.
    Though I oft intend
    All my ways to mend,
Though I oft intend, strength fails ay.
The sair assaults of sin prevails ay.

What shall I say? Are all my pleasures past?
Shall worldly lusts now take their leave at last?
  Yea, Christ, these earthly toys
  Shall turn to heavenly joys.
    Let the world be gone,
    I'll love Christ alone!
Let the world be gone—I care not.
Christ is my love alone—I fear not.

～

EDMUND SPENSER
(*ca.* 1552–1599)

Much of Spenser's poetry is dominated by the Renaissance predilection for l'amour courtois, *but on the occasions when his Christianity holds sway the results are sublime.*

From *The Faerie Queene*, II, Canto VIII

And is there care in heaven? and is there love
   In heavenly spirits to these creatures base
That may compassion of their evils move?
   There is: else much more wretched were the case
   Of men, than beasts. But, O! th' exceeding grace
Of highest God, that loves his creatures so,
   And all his works with mercy doth embrace,
That blessed angels he sends to and fro,
To serve to wicked man, to serve his wicked foe.

How oft do they their silver bowers leave,
   To come to succour us, that succour want?
How oft do they with golden pinions cleave
   The flitting skies, like flying pursuivant,
   Against foul fiends to aid us militant?
They for us fight, they watch and duly ward,
   And their bright squadrons round about us plant,
And all for love, and nothing for reward:
O! why should heavenly God to men have such regard?

From *Amoretti*

Most glorious Lord of life! that, on this day,
Didst make thy triumph over death and sin;
And, having harrowed hell, didst bring away
Captivity thence captive, us to win:
This joyous day, dear Lord, with joy begin;
And grant that we, for whom thou didest die,
Being with thy dear blood clean washed from sin,
May live for ever in felicity!
And that thy love we weighing worthily,
May likewise love thee for the same again;
And for thy sake, that all like dear didst buy,
With love may one another entertain:
So let us love, dear Love, like as we ought;
Love is the lesson which the Lord us taught.

From *An Hymne of Heavenly Love*

Love, lift me up upon thy golden wings,
From this base world unto thy heaven's height,
Where I may see those admirable things,
Which there thou workest by thy sovereign might,
Far above feeble reach of earthly sight,
That I thereof an heavenly Hymn may sing
Unto the God of Love, high heaven's king.

Many lewd layes (ah woe is me the more)
In praise of that mad fit, which fools call love,
I have in th'heat of youth made heretofore,
That in light wits did loose affection move.
But all those follies now I do reprove,
And turned have the tenor of my string,
The heavenly praises of true love to sing.

And ye that want with greedy vain desire
To read my fault, and wondering at my flame,
To warm yourselves at my wide sparkling fire,

Sith now that heat is quenched, quench my blame,
And in her ashes shroud my dying shame:
For who my passed follies now pursues,
Begins his own, and my old fault renews.

Before this world's great frame, in which all things
Are now contained, found any being place,
Ere flitting Time could wag his eyas wings
About that mighty bound, which doth embrace
The rolling Spheres, and parts their hours by space,
That high eternal power, which now doth move
In all these things, moved in itself in love.

It loved itself, because itself was fair;
(For fair is loved;) and of itself begot
Like to itself his eldest son and heir,
Eternal, pure, and void of sinful blot,
The firstling of his joy, in whom no iot
Of loves dislike, or pride was to be found,
Whom he therefore with equal honour crowned.

With him he reigned, before all time prescribed,
In endless glory and immortal might,
Together with that third from them derived,
Most wise, most holy, most almighty Spright,
Whose kingdom's throne no thought of earthly wight
Can comprehend, much less my trembling verse
With equal words can hope it to rehearse.

Yet O most blessed Spirit, pure lamp of light,
Eternal spring of grace and wisdom true,
Vouchsafe to shed into my barren spright,
Some little drop of thy celestial dew,
That may my rhymes with sweet infuse embrew,
And give my words equal unto my thought,
To tell the marvels by thy mercy wrought.

* * *

And look at last how of most wretched wights,
He taken was, betrayed, and false accused,
How with most scornful taunts, and fell despites
He was reviled, disgraced, and foul abused,
How scourged, how crowned, how buffeted, how bruised;
And lastly how twixt robbers crucified,
With bitter wounds through hands, through feet and side.

Then let thy flinty heart that feels no pain,
Empierced be with pitiful remorse,
And let thy bowels bleed in every vein,
At sight of his most sacred heavenly corse,
So torn and mangled with malicious force,
And let thy soul, whose sins his sorrows wrought,
Melt into tears, and groan in grieved thought.

With sense whereof whilest so thy softened spirit
Is inly touched, and humbled with meek zeal,
Through meditation of his endless merit,
Lift up thy mind to th'author of thy weal,
And to his sovereign mercy do appeal;
Learn him to love, that loved thee so dear,
And in thy breast his blessed image bear.

With all thy heart, with all thy soul and mind,
Thou must him love, and his behests embrace:
All other loves, with which the world doth blind
Weak fancies, and stir up affections base,
Thou must renounce, and utterly displace,
And give thyself unto him full and free,
That full and freely gave himself to thee.

Then shalt thou feel thy spirit so possessed,
And ravished with devouring great desire
Of his dear self, that shall thy feeble breast
Inflame with love, and set thee all on fire
With burning zeal, through every part entire,
That in no earthly thing thou shalt delight,
But in his sweet and amiable sight.

Thenceforth all world's desire will in thee die,
And all earth's glory on which men do gaze,
Seem dirt and dross in thy pure sighted eye,
Compared to that celestial beauty's blaze,
Whose glorious beams all fleshly sense doth daze
With admiration of their passing light,
Blinding the eyes and lumining the spright.

Then shall thy ravished soul inspired be
With heavenly thoughts, far above human skill,
And thy bright radiant eyes shall plainly see
Th'Idea of his pure glory present still,
Before thy face, that all thy spirits shall fill
With sweet enragement of celestial love,
Kindled through sight of those fair things above.

From *An Hymne of Heavenly Beautie*

Ne from thenceforth doth any fleshly sense,
Or idle thought of earthly things remain,
But all that earst seemed sweet, seems now offence,
And all that pleased earst, now seems to pain.
Their joy, their comfort, their desire, their gain,
Is fixed all on that which now they see,
All other sights but feigned shadows be.

And that fair lamp, which useth to enflame
The hearts of men with self consuming fire,
Thenceforth seems foul, and full of sinful blame;
And all that pomp, to which proud minds aspire
By name of honour, and so much desire,
Seems to them baseness, and all riches dross,
And all mirth sadness, and all lucre loss.

So full their eyes are of that glorious sight,
And senses fraught with such satiety,
That in nought else on earth they can delight,
But in th'aspect of that felicity,
Which they have written in their inward eye;

On which they feed, and in their fastened mind
All happy joy and full contentment find.

Ah then my hungry soul, which long hast fed
On idle fancies of thy foolish thought,
And with false beauties flattering bait misled,
Hast after vain deceitful shadows sought,
Which all are fled, and now have left thee nought,
But late repentance through thy follies prief;
Ah cease to gaze on matter of thy grief.

And look at last up to that sovereign light,
From whose pure beams all perfect beauty springs,
That kindleth love in every godly spright,
Even the love of God, which loathing brings
Of this vile world, and these gay seeming things;
With whose sweet pleasures being so possessed,
Thy straying thoughts henceforth for ever rest.

~

BEN JONSON
(1573–1637)

*A contemporary of Shakespeare, Ben Jonson is best known as a drama-
tist. Yet, like Shakespeare, his lyric genius shines through his plays,
most notably in the 'Hymn to Diana' from* Cynthia's Revels *and in
the incomparable 'Song to Celia' from* Volpone, *beginning with the
immortal lines, 'Drink to me only with thine eyes, And I will pledge
with mine'. He is not so well known for his religious verse but his
'Hymn to God the Father' is a notable exception.*

A Hymn to God the Father

Hear me, O God!
   A broken heart
   Is my best part:
Use still thy rod,
   That I may prove
   Therein, thy love.

If thou hadst not
   Been stern to me,
   But left me free,
I had forgot
   Myself and thee.

For sin's so sweet,
   As minds ill bent
   Rarely repent,
Until they meet
   Their punishment:

Who more can crave
   Than thou hast done:
   That gav'st a Son,

To free a slave?
   First made of nought;
   With all since bought.

Sin, Death, and Hell,
   His glorious Name
   Quite overcame;
Yet I rebel,
   And slight the same.

But I'll come in,
   Before my loss,
   Me farther toss,
As sure to win
   Under His Cross.

~

JOHN DONNE
(1573–1631)

With Donne, whose muse on dromedary trots,
Wreathe iron pokers into true-love knots;
Rhyme's sturdy cripple, fancy's maze and clue,
Wit's forge and fire-blast, meaning's press and screw.

Samuel Taylor Coleridge

Donne is the antithesis of the scholastic.

T. S. Eliot

As the above words testify, T. S. Eliot believed that the works of John Donne represented a break with medieval tradition. Whether this is so it was certainly the case that Donne's robust defence of the Anglican Church placed him firmly on the side of the Reformers. Born in the same year as Ben Jonson, his life reflected in microcosm the great confusion in religious affairs which followed in the wake of the Reformation. Baptised as a Catholic and connected through his mother with St Thomas More, he switched his allegiance to the established Church when still a young man. Under the direction of Thomas Morton he commenced writing religious polemic against the Catholic Church. Yet his path from Catholicism to Anglicanism had not been without difficulty and the satirical 'The Progress of the Soul' (1601), with its disturbed scepticism, demonstrated a mind and heart in turmoil. It was not until his ordination into the Anglican ministry in 1614 that he finally reached a position of calm acceptance of his theological position, tempered by occasional doubt.

Holy Sonnets

I

As due by many titles I resign
My self to thee, O God, first I was made
By thee, and for thee, and when I was decay'd
The blood bought that, the which before was thine,
I am thy son, made with thy self to shine,
Thy servant, whose pains thou hast still repaid,
Thy sheep, thine Image, and till I betray'd
My self, a temple of thy Spirit divine;
Why doth the devil then usurp in me?
Why doth he steal, nay ravish that's thy right?
Except thou rise and for thine own work fight,
Oh I shall soon despair, when I do see
That thou lov'st mankind well, yet wilt not choose me.
And Satan hates me, yet is loth to lose me.

2

Oh my black Soul! Now thou art summoned
By sickness, death's herald, and champion;
Thou art like a pilgrim, which abroad hath done
Treason, and durst not turn to whence he is fled,
Or like a thief, which till death's doom be read,
Wisheth himself delivered from prison;
But damn'd and hal'd to execution,
Wisheth that still he might be imprisoned;
Yet grace, if thou repent, thou canst not lack;
But who shall give thee that grace to begin?
Oh make thy self with holy mourning black,
And red with blushing, as thou art with sin;
Or wash thee in Christ's blood, which hath this might
That being red, it dyes red souls to white.

3

This is my play's last scene, here heavens appoint
My pilgrimage's last mile; and my race
Idly, yet quickly run, hath this last pace,
My span's last inch, my minute's last point,
And gluttonous death, will instantly unjoint
My body, and soul, and I shall sleep a space,
But my ever-waking part shall see that face,
Whose fear already shakes my every joint:
Then, as my soul, to heaven her first seat, takes flight,
And earth-borne body, in the earth shall dwell,
So, fall my sins, that all may have their right,
To where they are bred, and would press me, to hell.
Impute me righteous, thus purged of evil,
For thus I leave the world, the flesh, and devil.

4

At the round earth's imagin'd corners, blow
Your trumpets, Angels, and arise, arise
From death, you numberless infinities
Of souls, and to your scattered bodies go,
All whom the flood did, and fire shall o'erthrow,
All whom war, dearth, age, agues, tyrannies,
Despair, law, chance, hath slain, and you whose eyes
Shall behold God, and never taste death's woe.
But let them sleep, Lord, and me mourn a space,
For, if above all these, my sins abound,
'Tis late to ask abundance of thy grace,
When we are there; here on this lowly ground,
Teach me how to repent; for that's as good
As if thou hadst seal'd my pardon, with thy blood.

5

If poisonous minerals, and if that tree,
Whose fruit threw death on else immortal us,
If lecherous goats, if serpents envious
Cannot be damn'd; Alas; why should I be?
Why should intent or reason, born in me,
Make sins, else equal, in me, more heinous?
And mercy being easy, and glorious
To God, in his stern wrath, why threatens he?
But who am I, that dare dispute with thee?
O God, Oh! of thine onely worthy blood,
And my tears, make a heavenly Lethean flood,
And drown in it my sins' black memory.
That thou remember them, some claim as debt,
I think it mercy, if thou wilt forget.

6

Death be not proud, though some have called thee
Mighty and dreadful, for, thou art not so,
For, those, whom thou think'st, thou dost overthrow,
Die not, poor death, nor yet canst thou kill me;
From rest and sleep, which but thy pictures be,
Much pleasure, then from thee, much more must flow,
And soonest our best men with thee do go,
Rest of their bones, and soul's delivery.
Thou art slave to Fate, chance, kings, and desperate men,
And dost with poison, war, and sickness dwell,
And poppy, or charms can make us sleep as well,
And better than thy stroke; why swell'st thou then?
One short sleep past, we wake eternally,
And death shall be no more, Death thou shalt die.

Batter my heart, three person'd God; for, you
As yet but knock, breathe, shine, and seek to mend;
That I may rise, and stand, o'erthrow me, and bend
Your force, to break, blow, burn and make me new.
I, like an usurpt town, to another due,
Labour to admit you, but Oh, to no end,
Reason, your viceroy in me, me should defend,
But is captiv'd, and proves weak or untrue.
Yet dearly I love you, and would be lov'd fain,
But am betroth'd unto your enemy,
Divorce me, untie, or break that knot again,
Take me to you, imprison me, for I
Except you enthrall me, never shall be free,
Nor ever chaste, except you ravish me.

Good Friday, 1613. Riding Westward

Let man's Soul be a Sphere, and then, in this,
The intelligence that moves, devotion is,
And as the other Spheres, by being grown
Subject to foreign motions, lose their own.
And being by others hurried every day,
Scarce in a year their natural form obey:
Pleasure or business, so, our Souls admit
For their first mover, and are whirled by it.
Hence is't, that I am carried towards the West
This day, when my Soul's form bends toward the East.
There I should see a Sun, by rising set,
And by that setting endless day beget;
But that Christ on this Cross, did rise and fall,
Sin had eternally benighted all.
Yet dare I almost be glad, I do not see
That spectacle of too much weight for me.
Who sees God's face, that is self life, must die;

What a death were it then to see God die?
It made his own Lieutenant Nature shrink,
It made his footstool crack, and the Sun wink.
Could I behold those hands which span the Poles,
And tune all spheres at once, pierc'd with those holes?
Could I behold that endless height which is
Zenith to us, and to our Antipodes,
Humbled below us? Or that blood which is
The seat of all our Souls, if not of his,
Make dirt of dust, or that flesh which was worn
By God, for his apparel, rag'd and torn?
If on these things I durst not look, durst I
Upon his miserable mother cast mine eye,
And was God's partner here, and furnish'd thus
Half of that Sacrifice, which ransom'd us?
Though these things, as I ride, be from mine eye,
They are present yet unto my memory,
For that looks towards them; and thou look'st towards me,
O Saviour, as thou hang'st upon the tree;
I turn my back to thee, but to receive
Corrections, till thy mercies bid thee leave.
O think me worth thine anger, punish me,
Burn off my rusts, and my deformity,
Restore thine Image, so much, by thy grace,
That thou may'st know me, and I'll turn my face.

A Hymn to Christ, at the
Author's Last Going into Germany

In what torn ship soever I embark,
That ship shall be my emblem of thy Ark;
What sea soever swallow me, that flood
Shall be to me an emblem of thy blood;
Though thou with clouds of anger do disguise
Thy face; yet through that mask I know those eyes,
    Which, though they turn away sometimes,
        They never will despise.

I sacrifice this Island unto thee,
And all whom I lov'd there, and who lov'd me;
When I have put our seas twixt them and me,
Put thou thy sea betwixt my sins and thee.
As the tree's sap doth seek the root below
In winter, in my winter now I go,
    Where none but thee, th'Eternal root
        Of true Love I may know.

Nor thou nor thy religion dost control,
The amorousness of an harmonious Soul,
But thou would'st have that love thy self: As thou
Art jealous, Lord, so I am jealous now,
Thou lov'st not, till from loving more, thou free
My soul: Who ever gives, takes liberty:
    O, if thou car'st not whom I love
        Alas, thou lov'st not me.

Seal then this bill of my Divorce to All,
On whom those fainter beams of love did fall;
Marry those loves, which in youth scattered be
On Fame, Wit, Hopes (false mistresses) to thee.
Churches are best for Prayer, that have least light:
To see God only, I go out of sight:
    And to scape stormy days, I choose
        An Everlasting night.

GEORGE HERBERT
(1593–1633)

*George Herbert was the son of Lady Magdalen Herbert, to whom
Donne addressed his* Holy Sonnets. *Like Donne, Herbert took Angli-
can orders. In both his life and works he represents the early flowering
of that Anglo-Catholicism which was being championed in his day by
William Laud. He died in the same year that Laud, later to be be-
headed for endeavouring 'to overthrow the Protestant religion', became
Archbishop of Canterbury.*

Easter

I got me flowers to straw Thy way,
  I got me boughs off many a tree;
But Thou was up by break of day,
  And brought'st Thy sweets along with Thee.

Yet though my flowers be lost, they say
  A heart can never come too late;
Teach it to sing Thy praise this day,
  And then this day my life shall date.

The Agonie

Philosophers have measur'd mountains,
Fathom'd the depths of seas, of states, and kings,
Walk'd with a staff to heav'n, and traced fountains:
  But there are two vast, spacious things,
The which to measure it doth more behove:
Yet few there are that sound them; Sin and Love.

Who would know Sin, let him repair
Unto Mount Olivet; there shall he see

A man so wrung with pains, that all his hair,
    His skin, his garments bloody be.
Sin is that press and vice, which forceth pain
To hunt his cruel food through ev'ry vein.

    Who knows not Love, let him assay
And taste that juice, which on the cross a pike
Did set again abroach; then let him say
    If ever he did taste the like.
Love is that liquour sweet and most divine,
Which my God feels as blood; but I, as wine.

Vanitie

    The fleet Astronomer can bore,
And thread the spheres with his quick-piercing mind:
He views their stations, walks from door to door,
    Surveys, as if he had design'd
To make a purchase there: he sees their dances,
        And knoweth long before
Both their full ey'd aspects, and secret glances.

    The nimble Diver with his side
Cuts through the working waves, that he may fetch
His dearly-earned pearl, which God did hide
    On purpose from the ventrous wretch;
That he might save his life, and also hers,
        Who with excessive pride
Her own destruction and his danger wears.

    The subtle Chymick can devest
And strip the creature naked, till he find
The callow principles within their nest:
    There he imparts to them his minde,
Admitted to their bed-chamber, before
        They appear trim and drest
To ordinary suitors at the door.

What hath not man sought out and found,
But his dear God? who yet his glorious law
Embosoms in us, mellowing the ground
    With showers and frosts, with love and aw,
So that we need not say, Where's this command?
      Poor man, thou searchest round
To find out *death*, but missest *life* at hand.

Vertue

Sweet day, so cool, so calm, so bright,
The bridal of the earth and sky:
The dew shall weep thy fall tonight;
    For thou must die.

Sweet rose, whose hue angry and brave
Bids the rash gazer wipe his eye:
Thy root is ever in its grave,
    And thou must die.

Sweet spring, full of sweet days and roses,
A box where sweets compacted lie;
My music shows ye have your closes,
    And all must die.

Only a sweet and virtuous soul,
Like season'd timber, never gives;
But though the whole world turn to coal,
    Then chiefly lives.

The Pulley

    When God at first made man,
Having a glass of blessings standing by;
Let us (said he) pour on him all we can;
Let the world's riches, which dispersed lie,
   Contract into a span.

    So strength first made a way;
Then beauty flow'd, then wisdom, honour, pleasure:

When almost all was out, God made a stay,
Perceiving that alone of all his treasure
   Rest in the bottom lay.

   For if I should (said he)
Bestow this jewel also on my creature,
He would adore my gifts instead of me,
And rest in Nature, not the God of Nature:
   So both should losers be.

   Yet let him keep the rest,
But keep them with repining restlessness:
Let him be rich and weary, that at least,
If goodness lead him not, yet weariness
   May toss him to my breast.

Love

Love bade me welcome: yet my soul drew back,
   Guilty of dust and sin.
But quick-ey'd Love, observing me grow slack
   From my first entrance in,
Drew nearer to me, sweetly questioning,
   If I lack'd anything.

A guest, I answer'd, worthy to be here:
   Love said, You shall be he.
I the unkind, ungrateful? Ah my dear,
   I cannot look on thee.
Love took my hand, and smiling did reply,
   Who made the eyes but I?

Truth Lord, but I have marr'd them: let my shame
   Go where it doth deserve.
And know you not, says Love, who bore the blame?
   My dear, then I will serve.
You must sit down, says Love, and taste my meat:
   So I did sit and eat.

Peace

Sweet Peace, where dost thou dwell? I humbly crave,
    Let me once know.
  I sought thee in a secret cave,
    And asked if Peace were there.
A hollow wind did seem to answer, 'No;
    Go seek elsewhere.'

I did; and going did a rainbow note;
    Surely, thought I,
  This is the lace of Peace's coat,
    I will search out the matter.
But while I looked, the clouds immediately
    Did break and scatter.

Then went I to a garden, and did spy
    A gallant flower,
  The Crown Imperial. Sure, said I,
    Peace at the root must dwell.
But when I digged, I saw a worm devour
    What showed so well.

At length I met a reverend good old man,
    Whom when for Peace
  I did demand, he thus began:
    'There was a Prince of old
At Salem dwelt. Who lived with good increase
    Of flock and fold.

'He sweetly lived; yet sweetness did not save
    His life from foes.
  But after death out of His grave
    There sprang twelve stalks of wheat;
Which many wondering at, got some of those
    To plant and set.

'It prospered strangely, and did soon disperse
    Through all the earth;

For they that taste it do rehearse
    That virtue lies therein;
A secret virtue, bringing peace and mirth
    By flight of sin.

'Take of this grain, which in my garden grows,
    And grows for you;
  Make bread of it; and that repose
    And peace, which everywhere
With so much earnestness you do pursue,
    Is only there.'

~

THOMAS RANDOLPH
(1605–1635)

In his short life Thomas Randolph gained an extraordinary reputation both as poet and playwright, helped and encouraged by Ben Jonson whom he befriended.

An Elegie

Love, give me leave to serve thee, and be wise,
To keep thy torch in, but restore blind eyes.
I will a flame into my bosom take,
That Martyrs Court when they embrace the stake:
Not dull, and smoky fires, but heat divine,
That burns not to consume, but to refine.
I have a Mistress for perfections rare
In every eye, but in my thoughts most fair.
Like Tapers on the Altar shine her eyes;
Her breath is the perfume of Sacrifice.
And whereso'ere my fancy would begin,
Still her perfection lets religion in.
I touch her like my Beads with devout care;
And come unto my Courtship as my Prayer.
We sit, and talk, and kiss away the hours,
As chastely as the morning dews kiss flowers.
Go wanton Lover spare thy sighs and tears,
Put on the Livery which thy dotage wears,
And call it Love, where heresy gets in
Zeal's but a coal to kindle greater sin.
We wear no flesh, but one another greet,
As blessed souls in separation meet.
Were't possible that my ambitious sin,
Durst commit rapes upon a *Cherubin*,
I might have lustful thoughts to her, of all

Earth's heav'nly Choir, the most Angelical.
Looking into my breast, her form I find
That like my Guardian-Angel keeps my mind
From rude attempts; and when affections stir,
I calm all passions with one thought of her.
Thus they whose reason's love, and not their sense,
The spirits love: thus one Intelligence
Reflects upon his like, and by chaste loves
In the same sphere this and that Angel moves.
Nor is this barren Love; one noble thought
Begets another, and that still is brought
To bed of more; virtues and grace increase,
And such a numerous issue ne're can cease.
Where Children, though great blessings, only be
Pleasures repriv'd to some posterity.
Beasts love like men, if men in lust delight,
And call that Love which is but appetite.
When essence meets with essence, and souls join
in mutual knots, that's the true Nuptial twine:
Such Lady is my Love, and such is true;
All other Love is to your Sex, not You.

~

EDMUND WALLER
(1606–1687)

*As with so many of his contemporaries, Edmund Waller became em-
broiled in the volatile politics of this turbulent period in English history.
A staunch Royalist at the time of the Civil War, he was involved in a
conspiracy against Parliament which became known as 'Waller's plot'.
He was arrested and avoided execution, unlike his fellow conspirators,
by abject confession and the payment of a fine of £10,000. He was
banished from the realm and lived in exile in France until the banish-
ment was revoked in 1651. In this verse, written in old age, he takes
a tranquil look at his life in retrospect.*

Of the Last Verses in the Book

When we for Age could neither read nor write,
The Subject made us able to indite.
The Soul with Nobler Resolutions deckt,
The Body stooping, does Herself erect:
No Mortal parts are requisite to raise
Her, that Unbody'd can her Maker praise.

The Seas are quiet, when the Winds give o're;
So calm are we, when Passions are no more:
For then we know how vain it was to boast
Of fleeting Things, so certain to be lost.
Clouds of Affection from our younger Eyes
Conceal that emptiness, which Age descries.

The Soul's dark Cottage, batter'd and decay'd,
Lets in new Light thro chinks that time has made.
Stronger by weakness, wiser Men become
As they draw near to their Eternal home:
Leaving the Old, both Worlds at once they view,
That stand upon the Threshold of the New.

JOHN MILTON
(1608–1674)

Milton, like Edmund Waller, was involved in the intrigues of the Civil War. His sympathies, however, were entirely with the opposing side and he took up the Parliamentary cause with revolutionary zeal. Following Cromwell's victory, he supported and defended the execution of King Charles and became the official apologist for the Commonwealth in the years after the war. He was in the middle of writing Paradise Lost *at the time of the Restoration, which he strongly opposed, and the pessimism which the collapse of the Commonwealth engendered may have induced the despairing tone of much of his later work. Perhaps it is no coincidence that the early books of* Paradise Lost, *written before the Restoration, reflect the triumph of the godly whereas the last books are tinged with despair.*

Milton strayed so far from orthodox Christianity that Protestant critics have added their plaintive voices to those of their Catholic counterparts in criticising the heterodox nature of his views, expressed most candidly in his prose work De Doctrina Christiana *but also in* Paradise Regained *and* Samson Agonistes. *In* Paradise Regained *the figure of Christ is Puritanised to such a degree that he is transformed from a redeemer into a sublime stoic, almost as though Milton was making Christ in his own image. Of course, this does not detract from Milton's greatness as a poet nor from the genuine nature of his Christian faith, as expressed in his early verse.*

On Time

Fly, envious Time, till thou run out thy race,
Call on the lazy, leaden-stepping hours,
Whose speed is but the heavy plummet's pace,
And glut thyself with what thy womb devours,
Which is no more than what is false and vain,

And merely mortal dross;
So little is our loss,
So little is thy gain.
For when as each thing bad thou has entombed,
And last of all thy greedy self consumed,
Then long Eternity shall greet our bliss
With an individual kiss,
And joy shall overtake us as a flood;
When every thing that is sincerely good
And perfectly divine,
With Truth, and Peace, and Love shall ever shine,
About the supreme throne
Of Him, t'whose happy-making sight alone
When once our heavenly-guided soul shall climb,
Then, all this earthly grossness quit,
Attired with stars we shall for ever sit
    Triumphing over Death, and Chance, and thee, O Time.

At a Solemn Music

Blest pair of Sirens, pledges of Heaven's joy,
Sphere-born harmonious sisters, Voice and Verse
Wed your divine sounds; and mixed power employ
Dead things with inbreathed sense able to pierce,
And to our high-raised phantasy present
That undisturbed song of pure consent,
Ay sung before the sapphire-coloured throne
To Him that sits thereon,
With saintly shout and solemn jubilee;
Where the bright seraphim in burning row
Their loud uplifted angel-trumpets blow,
And the cherubic host in thousand quires
Touch their immortal harps of golden wires,
With those just spirits that wear victorious palms,
Hymns devout and holy psalms
Singing everlastingly;

That we on earth with undiscording voice
May rightly answer that melodious noise:
As once we did, till disproportioned sin
Jarred against nature's chime, and with harsh din
Broke the fair music that all creatures made
To their great Lord; whose love their motion swayed
In perfect diapason, whilst they stood
In first obedience and their state of good.
O may we soon again renew that song,
And keep in tune with Heaven, till God ere long
To His celestial consort us unite,
To live with Him, and sing in endless morn of light.

On the Religious Memory
of Mrs Catherine Thomson,
My Christian Friend,
Deceased December 16, 1646

When Faith and Love, which parted from thee never,
　　Had ripened thy just soul to dwell with God,
　　Meekly thou didst resign this earthly load
　　Of Death, called Life, which us from Life doth sever.
Thy works, and alms, and all thy good endeavour,
　　Stayed not behind, nor in the grave were trod;
　　But, as Faith pointed with her golden rod,
　　Followed thee up to joy and bliss for ever.
Love led them on; and Faith, who knew them best
　　Thy handmaids, clad them o'er with purple beams
　　And azure wings, that up they flew so drest,
And spake the truth of thee on glorious themes
　　Before the Judge; who thenceforth bid thee rest,
　　And drink thy fill of pure immortal streams.

SIDNEY GODOLPHIN
(1610–1643)

Sidney Godolphin joined the King's forces on the outbreak of war and was killed in a skirmish at Chagford in Devon. Although he died young, he left several poems of note to posterity, not least of which is this 'Hymn'.

Hymn

Lord when the wise men came from far,
Led to thy Cradle by a Star,
Then did the shepherds too rejoice,
Instructed by thy Angels' voice:
Blest were the wise men in their skill,
And shepherds in their harmless will.

Wise men in tracing Nature's laws
Ascend unto the highest cause,
Shepherds with humble fearfulness
Walk safely, though their light be less:
Though wise men better know the way
It seems no honest heart can stray.

There is no merit in the wise
But love, (the shepherds' sacrifice).
Wise men all ways of knowledge past,
To th'shepherds wonder come at last:
To know, can only wonder breed,
And not to know, is wonder's seed.

A wise man at the Altar bows
And offers up his studied vows
And is received; may not the tears,
Which spring too from a shepherd's fears,

And sighs upon his frailty spent,
Though not distinct, be eloquent?

'Tis true, the object sanctifies
All passions which within us rise,
But since no creature comprehends
The cause of causes, end of ends,
He who himself vouchsafes to know
Best pleases his creator so.

When then our sorrows we apply
To our own wants and poverty,
When we look upon in all distress
And our own misery confess,
Sending both thanks and prayers above,
Then though we do not know, we love.

~

ANNE BRADSTREET
(1612–1672)

Anne Dudley was probably born in Northampton, marrying Simon Bradstreet in 1628. As Puritans the newly-weds escaped persecution in England by emigrating to the New World in 1630. Although her husband eventually became governor of Massachusetts, it is Anne who is most remembered to posterity as the first American woman writer.

To My Dear and Loving Husband

If ever two were one, then surely we.
If ever man were lov'd by wife, then thee;
If ever wife was happy in a man,
Compare with me ye women if you can.
I prize thy love more than whole mines of gold,
Or all the riches that the East doth hold.
My love is such that rivers cannot quench,
Nor aught but love from thee, give recompense.
Thy love is such I can no way repay,
The heavens reward thee manifold, I pray.
Then while we live, in love lets so persever
That, when we live no more, we may live ever.

Before the Birth of One of Her Children

All things within this fading world hath end,
Adversity doth still our joys attend;
No ties so strong, no friends so dear and sweet,
But with death's parting blow is sure to meet.
The sentence past is most irrevocable,
A common thing, yet oh inevitable.
How soon, my Dear, death may my steps attend,
How soon't may be thy Lot to lose thy friend,
We are both ignorant, yet love bids me
These farewell lines to recommend to thee,
That when that knot's untied that made us one,
I may seem thine, who in effect am none.
And if I see not half my dayes that's due,
What nature would, God grant to yours and you;
The many faults that well you know I have
Let be interr'd in my oblivious grave;
If any worth or virtue were in me,
Let that live freshly in thy memory
And when thou feel'st no grief, as I no harms,
Yet love thy dead, who long lay in thine arms.
And when thy loss shall be repaid with gains
Look to my little babes, my dear remains.
And if thou love thyself; or loved'st me,
These o protect from step Dames injury.
And if chance to thine eyes shall bring this verse.
With some sad sighs honour my absent Herse;
And kiss this paper for thy loves dear sake,
Who with salt tears this last Farewel did take.

In Memory of My Dear Grandchild
Elizabeth Bradstreet,
Who Deceased August, 1665,
being a Year and a Half Old

Farewell dear babe, my heart's too much content,
Farewell sweet babe, the pleasure of mine eye,
Farewell fair flower that for a space was lent,
Then ta'en away unto Eternity.
Blest babe, why should I once bewail thy fate,
Or sigh thy days so soon were terminate,
Sith thou art settled in an Everlasting state?

By nature trees do rot when they are grown,
And plums and apples thoroughly ripe do fall,
And corn and grass are in their season mown,
And time brings down what is both strong and tall.
But plants new set to be eradicate,
And buds new blown to have so short a date,
Is by His hand alone that guides nature and fate.

~

After the Winter

As spring the winter doth succeed
And leaves the naked trees do dress,
The earth all black is clothed in green.
At sunshine each their joy express.

My sun's returned with healing wings,
My soul and body doth rejoice,
My heart exults and praises sings
To him that heard my wailing voice.

My winter's past, my storms are gone,
And former clouds seem now all fled,
But if they must eclipse again,
I'll run where I was succoured.

I have a shelter from the storm,
A shadow from the fainting heat,
I have access unto his throne,
Who is a God so wondrous great.

O hath thou made my pilgrimage
Thus pleasant, fair, and good,
Blessed me in youth and elder age,
My Baca made a springing flood.

O studious am what I shall do
To show my duty with delight;
All I can give is but thine own
And at the most a simple mite.

RICHARD CRASHAW
(*ca.* 1613–1649)

Richard Crashaw was born in London, the only son of the Puritan poet and clergyman William Crashaw. About 1636 he became a Fellow of Peterhouse which had become the centre of Laudian High Churchmanship in Cambridge. In 1643, the visitation of the Parliamentary Commission had stripped the chapel at Peterhouse and broken down 'Superstitious Pictures' in Little St Mary's, where Crashaw was based. In the following year he lost his fellowship for refusing to take the Covenant. He left Cambridge and soon afterwards became a Roman Catholic, living in exile in Paris. He lived in relative poverty and great distress in Paris and Rome before being appointed to the post of subcanon at the Cathedral of Loreto in April 1649. He died four months later. As well as being the author of many English poems, Crashaw published a noted volume of Latin verse, Epigrammatum Sacrorum Liber, *which contains the famous line on the miracle at Cana:* 'Nympha pudica Deum vidit et erubuit' (*the modest water saw its God and blushed*).

The Author's Motto

Live Jesus, Live, and let it be
My life to die, for love of thee.

Charitas Nimia, or The Dear Bargain

Lord, what is man? why should he cost thee
   So dear? what had his ruin lost thee?
Lord, what is man, that thou hast over-bought
   So much a thing of nought?

Love is too kind, I see, and can
Make but a simple Merchant man;
'Twas for such sorry merchandise
Bold Painters have put out his eyes.
Alas sweet Lord, what were't to thee
If there were no such worms as we?
     Heav'n ne're the less still Heav'n would be,
     Should mankind dwell
     In the deep hell,
   What have his woes to do with thee?
    Let him go weep
    O'er his own wounds;
    Seraphims will not sleep
Nor Spheres let fall their faithful rounds;
   Still would the youthful Spirits sin,
   And still thy spacious Palace ring:
Still would those beautious ministers of light
     Burn all as bright,
   And bow their flaming heads before thee;
Still Thrones and Dominations would adore thee;
Still would those ever-wakeful sons of fire
     Keep warm thy praise
     Both nights and days,
And teach thy lov'd name to their noble Lyre.
   Let froward dust then do its kind,
And give itself for sport to the proud wind;
Why should a piece of peevish clay plead shares
In the Eternity of thy old cares?
Why shouldst thou bow thy awful breast to see
What mine own madnesses have done with me?

Should not the King still keep his Throne
Because some desperate fool's undone?
Or will the world's illustrious eyes
Weep for every worm that dies?
   Will the gallant Sun
   E're the less glorious run?
Will he hang down his Golden head,
Or e're the sooner seek his western bed,
    Because some foolish fly
    Grows wanton, and will die?
If I was lost in misery,
What was it to thy heav'n and thee?
What was it to thy precious blood
If My foul heart call'd for a flood?
What if my faithless soul and I
    Would needs fall in
    With guilt and sin?
What did the Lamb, that he should die?
What did the Lamb, that he should need,
When the Wolf sins, himself to bleed?
   If my base lust
Bargain'd with death, and well-beseeming dust;
    Why should the white
    Lamb's bosom write
    The purple name
    Of my sin's shame?
Why should his unstain'd breast make good
My blushes with his own Heart-blood?

O my Saviour, make me see,
How dearly thou hast paid for me,
That Lost again my life may prove,
As then in Death, so now in Love.

A Hymn to the Name and Honour
of the Admirable Saint Teresa

Love, thou art absolute, sole Lord
Of life and death. To prove the word,
We'll now appeal to none of all
Those thy old soldiers, great and tall,
Ripe men of martyrdom, that could reach down
With strong arms their triumphant crown:
Such as could with lusty breath
Speak loud, unto the face of death,
Their great Lord's glorious name; to none
Of those whose spacious bosoms spread a throne
For love at large to fill. Spare blood and sweat:
We'll see Him take a private seat,
And make His mansion in the mild
And milky soul of a soft child.

Scarce has she learnt to lisp a name
Of martyr, yet she thinks it shame
Life should so long play with that breath
Which spent can buy so brave a death.
She never undertook to know
What death with love should have to do.
Nor has she e'er yet understood
Why, to show love, she should shed blood;
Yet, though she cannot tell you why,
She can love, and she can die.
Scarce has she blood enough to make
A guilty sword blush for her sake;
Yet has she a heart dares hope to prove
How much less strong is death than love . . .

Since 'tis not to be had at home,
She'll travel for a martyrdom.
No home for her, confesses she,
But where she may a martyr be.

She'll to the Moors, and trade with them
For this unvalued diadem;
She offers them her dearest breath,
With Christ's name in 't, in change for death:
She'll bargain with them, and will give
Them God, and teach them how to live
In Him; or, if they this deny,
For Him she'll teach them how to die.
So shall she leave amongst them sown
Her Lord's blood, or at least her own.

Farewell then, all the world, adieu!
Teresa is no more for you.
Farewell all pleasures, sports, and joys,
Never till now esteemed toys!
Farewell whatever dear may be—
Mother's arms, or father's knee!
Farewell house, and farewell home!
She's for the Moors and Martyrdom.

Sweet, not so fast; lo! thy fair spouse,
Whom thou seek'st with so swift vows,
Calls thee back, and bids thee come
T' embrace a milder martyrdom . . .

O how oft shalt thou complain
Of a sweet and subtle pain!
Of intolerable joys!
Of a death, in which who dies
Loves his death, and dies again,
And would for ever be so slain;
And lives and dies, and knows not why
To live, but that he still may die!
How kindly will thy gentle heart
Kiss the sweetly-killing dart!
And close in his embraces keep
Those delicious wounds, that weep

Balsam, to heal themselves with thus,
When these thy deaths, so numerous,
Shall all at once die into one,
And melt thy soul's sweet mansion;
Like a soft lump of incense, hasted
By too hot a fire, and wasted
Into perfuming clouds, so fast
Shalt thou exhale to heaven at last
In a resolving sigh, and then,—
O what? Ask not the tongues of men.

Angels cannot tell; suffice,
Thyself shalt feel thine own full joys,
And hold them fast for ever there.
So soon as thou shalt first appear,
The moon of maiden stars, thy white
Mistress, attended by such bright
Souls as thy shining self, shall come,
And in her first ranks make thee room;
Where, 'mongst her snowy family,
Immortal welcomes wait for thee.
O what delight, when she shall stand
And teach thy lips heaven, with her hand,
On which thou now may'st to thy wishes
Heap up thy consecrated kisses!
What joy shall seize thy soul, when she,
Bending her blessed eyes on thee,
Those second smiles of heaven, shall dart
Her mild rays through thy melting heart!

Angels, thy old friends, there shall greet thee,
Glad at their own home now to meet thee.
All thy good works which went before,
And waited for thee at the door,
Shall own thee there; and all in one
Weave a constellation
Of crowns, with which the King, thy spouse,

Shall build up thy triumphant brows.
All thy old woes shall now smile on thee,
And thy pains sit bright upon thee:
All thy sorrows here shall shine,
And thy sufferings be divine,
Tears shall take comfort, and turn gems,
And wrongs repent to diadems.
Even thy deaths shall live, and new
Dress the soul which late they slew.
Thy wounds shall blush to such bright scars
As keep account of the Lamb's wars.

Those rare works, where thou shalt leave writ
Love's noble history, with wit
Taught thee by none but Him, while here
They feed our souls, shall clothe thine there.
Each heavenly word by whose hid flame
Our hard hearts shall strike fire, the same
Shall flourish on thy brows, and be
Both fire to us and flame to thee;
Whose light shall live bright in thy face
By glory, in our hearts by grace.
Thou shalt look round about, and see
Thousands of crown'd souls throng to be
Themselves thy crown, sons of thy vows,
The virgin-births with which thy spouse
Made fruitful thy fair soul; go now,
And with them all about thee bow
To Him; put on, He'll say, put on,
My rosy Love, that thy rich zone,
Sparkling with the sacred flames
Of thousand souls, whose happy names
Heaven keeps upon thy score: thy bright
Life brought them first to kiss the light
That kindled them to stars; and so
Thou with the Lamb, thy Lord, shalt go.

And, wheresoe'er He sets His white
Steps, walk with Him those ways of light,
Which who in death would live to see,
Must learn in life to die like thee.

Upon the Book and Picture of
the Seraphical Saint Teresa

O thou undaunted daughter of desires!
By all thy dower of lights and fires;
By all the eagle in thee, all the dove;
By all thy lives and deaths of love;
By thy large draughts of intellectual day,
And by thy thirsts of love more large than they;
By all thy brim-fill'd bowls of fierce desire,
By thy last morning's draught of liquid fire;
By the full kingdom of that final kiss
That seized thy parting soul, and seal'd thee His;
By all the Heav'n thou hast in Him
(Fair sister of the seraphim!);
By all of Him we have in thee;
Leave nothing of myself in me.
Let me so read thy life, that I
Unto all life of mine may die!

~

Verses from 'The Shepherd's Hymn'

We saw Thee in Thy balmy nest,
    Young dawn of our eternal day;
We saw Thine eyes break from the East,
    And chase the trembling shades away:
We saw Thee, and we blest the sight,
We saw Thee by Thine own sweet light.

Poor world, said I, what wilt thou do
    To entertain this starry stranger?
Is this the best thou canst bestow—
    A cold and not too cleanly manger?
Contend, the powers of heaven and earth,
To fit a bed for this huge birth.

Proud world, said I, cease your contest,
    And let the mighty Babe alone;
The phoenix builds the phoenix' nest,
    Love's architecture is His own.
The Babe, whose birth embraves this morn,
Made His own bed ere He was born.

I saw the curl'd drops, soft and slow,
    Come hovering o'er the place's head,
Off'ring their whitest sheets of snow,
    To furnish the fair infant's bed.
Forbear, said I, be not too bold;
Your fleece is white, but 'tis too cold.

I saw th' obsequious seraphim
    Their rosy fleece of fire bestow,
For well they now can spare their wings,
    Since Heaven itself lies here below.
Well done, said I; but arc you sure
Your down, so warm, will pass for pure?

No, no, your King's not yet to seek
    Where to repose His royal head;

See, see how soon His new-bloom'd cheek
   'Twixt mother's breasts is gone to bed!
Sweet choice, said we; no way but so,
Not to lie cold, yet sleep in snow!

She sings Thy tears asleep, and dips
   Her kisses in Thy weeping eye;
She spreads the red leaves of Thy lips,
   That in their buds yet blushing lie.
She 'gainst those mother diamonds tries
The points of her young eagle's eyes.

Welcome—tho' not to those gay flies,
   Gilded i' th' beams of earthly kings,
Slippery souls in smiling eyes—
   But to poor shepherds, homespun things,
Whose wealth's their flocks, whose wit's to be
Well read in their simplicity.

Yet, when young April's husband show'rs
   Shall bless the fruitful Maia's bed.
We'll bring the first-born of her flowers,
   To kiss Thy feet and crown Thy head.
To Thee, dread Lamb! whose love must keep
The shepherds while they feed their sheep.

To Thee, meek Majesty, soft King
   Of simple graces and sweet loves!
Each of us his lamb will bring,
   Each his pair of silver doves!
At last, in fire of Thy fair eyes,
Ourselves become our own best sacrifice!

On the Water of Our Lord's Baptism

Each blest drop, on each blest limb,
Is washt itself, in washing him:
Tis a Gem while it stays here,
While it falls hence 'tis a Tear.

But Men Loved Darkness Rather Than Light

The world's light shines; shine as it will,
The world will love its Darkness still:
I doubt though when the World's in Hell,
It will not love its Darkness half so well.

On St Peter Casting Away His
Nets at Our Saviour's Call

Thou hast the art on't Peter; and canst tell
    To cast thy Nets on all occasions well.
When Christ calls, and thy Nets would have thee stay:
    To cast them well's to cast them quite away.

I Am Not Worthy that Thou
Should'st Come under My Roof

Thy God was making haste into thy roof,
    Thy humble faith and fear keeps him aloof:
He'll be thy Guest, because he may not be,
    He'll come—into thy house? no, into thee.

Two Went up into the Temple to Pray

Two went to pray? o rather say
One went to brag, th'other to pray:

One stands up close and treads on high,
Where th'other dares not send his eye.

One nearer to God's altar trod,
The other to the Altar's God.

The Blind Cured by the Word of Our Saviour

Thou spak'st the word (thy word's a Law)
Thou spak'st and straight the blind man saw.

To speak and make the blind man see,
Was never man Lord spake like Thee.

To speak thus, was to speak (say I),
Not to his Ear, but to his Eye.

Christ Crucified

Thy restless feet now cannot go
     For us and our eternal good,
As they were ever wont. What though
     They swim, alas! in their own flood?

Thy hands to give Thou canst not lift,
     Yet will Thy hand still giving be;
It gives, but O, itself's the gift!
     It gives tho' bound, tho' bound 'tis free!

Upon Our Saviour's Tomb
Wherein Never Man Was Laid

How Life and Death in Thee
    Agree!
Thou had'st a virgin Womb
    And Tomb.
A Joseph did betroth
    Them both.

An Epitaph upon Husband and Wife

To these whom death again did wed
This grave's the second marriage-bed.
For though the hand of Fate could force
'Twixt soul and body a divorce,
It could not sever man and wife,
Because they both lived but one life.
Peace, good reader, do not weep;
Peace, the lovers are asleep.
They, sweet turtles, folded lie
In the last knot that love could tie.
Let them sleep, let them sleep on,
Till the stormy night be gone,
And the eternal morrow dawn;
Then the curtains will be drawn,
And they wake into a light
Whose day shall never die in night.

ABRAHAM COWLEY
(1618–1667)

In his own day, Cowley was considered the greatest of English poets, a judgment not shared by posterity. A staunch Royalist, he was forced from Cambridge at the same time as his friend Richard Crashaw. Like Crashaw, he went into exile to France, returning to England in 1654. His tribute to Crashaw, though displaying the differences between his own Anglican faith and Crashaw's Catholicism, is imbued with the deep Christian faith that both men shared.

On the Death of Mr Crashaw

Poet and Saint! To thee alone are given
The two most sacred Names of Earth and Heaven.
The hard and rarest Union which can be
Next that of Godhead with Humanity.
Long did the Muses banisht Slaves abide,
And built vain Pyramids to mortal pride;
Like Moses Thou (though Spell and Charms withstand)
Hast brought them nobly home back to the Holy Land.
    Ah wretched We, Poets of Earth! But Thou
Wert Living the same Poet which thou'rt Now.
Whilst Angels sing to thee their airs divine,
And joy in an applause so great as thine.
Equal society with them to hold,
Thou need'st not make new Songs, but say the Old.
And they (kind Spirits!) shall all rejoice to see
How little less than They, Exalted Man may be.
Still the old Heathen Gods in Numbers dwell,
The Heav'nliest thing on Earth still keeps up Hell.
Nor have we yet quite purg'd the Christian Land;
Still Idols here, like Calves at Bethel stand.

And though Pan's Death long since all Oracles broke,
Yet still in Rhyme the Fiend Apollo spoke:
Nay with the worst of Heathen dotage We
(Vain men!) the Monster Woman Deify;
Find Stars, and tie our Fates there in a Face,
And Paradise in them by whom we lost it, place.
What different faults corrupt our Muses thus?
Wanton as Girls, as old Wives, Fabulous!
   Thy spotless Muse, like Mary, did contain
The boundless Godhead; she did well disdain
That her eternal Verse employ'd should be
On a less subject than Eternity;
And for a sacred Mistress scorn'd to take,
But her whom God himself scorn'd not his Spouse to make.
It (in a kind) her Miracle did do;
A fruitful Mother was, and Virgin too.
How well (blest Swan) did Fate contrive thy death;
And made thee render up thy tuneful breath
In thy great Mistress' Arms? thou most divine
And richest Off'ring of Loretto's Shrine!
Where like some holy Sacrifice t'expire,
A Fever burns thee, and Love lights the Fire.
Angels (they say) brought the fam'd chapel there,
And bore the sacred Load in Triumph through the air.
'Tis surer much they brought thee there, and They,
And Thou, their charge, went singing all the way.
   Pardon, my Mother Church, if I consent
That Angels led him when from thee he went,
For even in Error sure no Danger is
When join'd with so much Piety as His.
Ah, mighty God, with shame I speak't, and grief,
Ah that our greatest Faults were in Belief!
And our weak Reason were ev'n weaker yet,
Rather than thus our Wills too strong for it.
His Faith perhaps in some nice Tenets might
Be wrong; his Life, I'm sure, was in the right.

And I myself a Catholic will be,
So far at least, great Saint, to Pray to thee.
  Hail, Bard Triumphant! and some care bestow
On us, the Poets Militant below!
Oppos'd by our old En'my, adverse Chance,
Attack'd by Envy, and by Ignorance,
Enchain'd by Beauty, tortur'd by Desires,
Expos'd by Tyrant-Love to savage Beasts and Fires.
Thou from low earth in nobler Flames didst rise,
And like Elijah, mount Alive the skies.
Elisha-like (but with a wish much less,
More fit thy Greatness, and my Littleness)
Lo here I beg (I whom thou once didst prove
So humble to Esteem, so Good to Love)
Not that thy Spirit might on me Doubled be,
I ask but Half thy mighty Spirit for Me.
And when my Muse soars with so strong a Wing,
'Twill learn of things Divine, and first of Thee to sing.

∽

HENRY VAUGHAN
(1622–1695)

Henry Vaughan, a devoted son of the Church of England, was an ardent Royalist who fought in the Civil War. His early secular verse is unremarkable and it wasn't until he underwent what is best described as a conversion experience that he began writing the sublime religious verse which is the foundation of his reputation. The cause of his conversion may have been linked with personal tragedies in his life such as the death of friends, including a brother, the defeat of the Royalist cause, and the near destruction of the Anglican Church. 'Certain Divine Rays break out of the Soul in adversity,' he wrote, 'like sparks of fire out of the afflicted flint.'

Peace

My soul, there is a country
   Far beyond the stars,
Where stands a winged sentry
   All skilful in the wars:
There, above noise and danger,
   Sweet Peace sits crown'd with smiles,
And One born in a manger
   Commands the beauteous files.
He is thy gracious Friend,
   And—O my soul, awake!—
Did in pure love descend
   To die here for thy sake.
If thou can get but thither,
   There grows the flower of Peace,
The Rose that cannot wither,
   Thy fortress, and thy ease.

Leave then thy foolish ranges;
 For none can thee secure
But One who never changes—
 Thy God, thy life, thy cure.

The Dawning

Ah! what time wilt thou come? when shall that cry
 The Bridegroom's Coming! fill the sky?
 Shall it in the Evening run
 When our words and works are done?
Or will thy all-surprising light
 Break at midnight?
When either sleep, or some dark pleasure
Possesseth mad man without measure;
Or shall these early, fragrant hours
 Unlock thy bowres?
And with their blush of light descry
Thy locks crown'd with eternity;
Indeed, it is the only time
That with thy glory doth best chime,
All now are stirring, ev'ry field
 Full hymns doth yield,
The whole Creation shakes off night,
And for thy shadow looks the light,
Stars now vanish without number;
Sleepy Planets set, and slumber,
The pursy Clouds disband, and scatter,
All expect some sudden matter,
Not one beam triumphs, but from far
 That morning-star;

O at what time soever thou
(Unknown to us,) the heavens wilt bow,
And, with thy Angels in the Van,
Descend to Judge poor careless man,

Grant, I may not like puddle lie
In a Corrupt security,
Where, if a traveller water crave,
He finds it dead, and in a grave;
But as this restless, vocal Spring
All day, and night doth run, and sing,
And though here born, yet is acquainted
Elsewhere, and flowing keeps untainted;
So let me all my busy age
In thy free services engage,
And though (while here) of force I must
Have Commerce sometimes with poor dust,
And in my flesh, though vile, and low,
As this doth in her Channel, flow,
Yet let my Course, my aim, my Love,
And chief acquaintance be above;
So when that day, and hour shall come
In which thy self will be the Sun,
Thou'lt find me drest and on my way,
Watching the Break of thy great day.

Cock-Crowing

Father of lights! what Sunny seed,
What glance of day hast thou confin'd
Into this bird? To all the breed
This busy Ray thou hast assign'd;
    Their magnetism works all night,
    And dreams of Paradise and light.

Their eyes watch for the morning hue,
Their little grain expelling night
So shines and sings, as if it knew
The path unto the house of light.
    It seems their candle, howe'r done,
    Was tinn'd and lighted at the sun.

If such a tincture, such a touch,
So firm a longing can empower

Shall thy own image think it much
To watch for thy appearing hour?
   If a mere blast so fill the sail,
   Shall not the breath of God prevail?

O thou immortal light and heat!
Whose hand so shines through all this frame,
That by the beauty of the seat,
We plainly see, who made the same.
   Seeing thy seed abides in me,
   Dwell thou in it, and I in thee.

To sleep without thee, is to die;
Yea, 'tis a death partakes of hell:
For where thou dost not close the eye
It never opens, I can tell.
   In such a dark, Egyptian border,
   The shades of death dwell and disorder.

If joys, and hopes, and earnest throws,
And hearts, whose Pulse beats still for light
Are given to birds; who, but thee, knows
A love-sick soul's exalted flight?
   Can souls be track'd by any eye
   But his, who gave them wings to fly?

Only this Veil which thou hast broke,
And must be broken yet in me,
This veil, I say, is all the cloak
And cloud which shadows thee from me.
   This veil thy full-ey'd love denies,
   And only gleams and fractions spies.

O take it off! make no delay,
But brush me with thy light, that I
May shine unto a perfect day,
And warm me at thy glorious Eye!
   O take it off! or till it flee,
   Though with no Lily, stay with me!

Quickness

False life! a foil and no more, when
    Wilt thou be gone?
Thou foul deception of all men
That would not have the true come on.

Thou art a Moon-like toil; a blind
    Self-posing state;
A dark contest of waves and wind;
A mere tempestuous debate.

Life is a fix'd, discerning light,
    A knowing joy;
No chance, or fit: but ever bright,
And calm and full, yet doth not cloy.

'Tis such a blissful thing, that still
    Doth vivify,
And shine and smile, and hath the skill
To please without Eternity.

Thou art a toilsome Mole, or less
    A moving mist
But life is, what none can express,
A quickness, which my God hath kissed.

The Revival

Unfold, unfold! Take in his light,
Who makes thy cares more short than night.
The joys, which with his day-star rise,
He deals to all but drowsy eyes;
And what the men of this world miss,
Some drops and dews of future bliss.
  Hark! How his winds have changed their note,
And with warm whispers call thee out.
The frosts are past, the storms are gone,
And backward life at last comes on.
The lofty groves in express joys
Reply unto the turtle's voice,
And here in dust and dirt, O here
The lilies of his love appear!

~

JOHN BUNYAN
(1628–1688)

Although noted principally as a writer of prose, no anthology of Christian verse would be complete without Bunyan's 'Pilgrim Song', or his short song of 'The Shepherd Boy'.

The Pilgrim Song

Who would true Valour see,
Let him come hither;
One here will Constant be,
Come Wind, come Weather.
There's no Discouragement
Shall make him once Relent
His first avow'd Intent
To be a Pilgrim.

Whoso beset him round
With dismal Stories,
Do but themselves Confound;
His strength the more is.
No Lion can him fright,
He'll with a Giant fight,
But he will have a right
To be a Pilgrim.

Hobgoblin, nor foul Fiend,
Can daunt his Spirit:
He knows, he at the end
Shall Life Inherit.
The Fancies fly away,
He'll fear not what men say,
He'll labour Night and Day
To be a Pilgrim.

The Shepherd Boy Sings in
the Valley of Humiliation

He that is down needs fear no fall,
  He that is low, no pride;
He that is humble ever shall
  Have God to be his guide.

I am content with what I have,
  Little be it or much:
And, Lord, contentment still I crave,
  Because Thou savest such.

Fullness to such a burden is
  That go on pilgrimage:
Here little, and hereafter bliss,
  Is best from age to age.

~

JOHN DRYDEN
(1631–1700)

Dryden, like so many of his contemporaries, was buffeted by the religious conflicts that plagued the seventeenth century. His family had been staunch Parliamentarians during the Civil War and his cousin, Sir Gilbert Pickering, was Cromwell's chamberlain, a fact which worked to the young Dryden's advantage when he came to London in 1657. His Heroic Stanzas *on Cromwell's death in 1658 marked the beginning of his literary career. Dryden modified his religious position over the years and his didactic poem,* Religio Laici, *published in 1682, argued the case for Anglicanism. His finest poem,* The Hind and the Panther, *published three years later, heralded his conversion to Roman Catholicism. Since his conversion coincided with the ascension to the throne of the avowedly Catholic James II, many have suspected that he had cynical motives in converting at this time, but the fact that he did not revert to the established Church when the Protestant William III usurped the throne in 1688 suggests otherwise. Certainly* The Hind and the Panther *appears to bear the hallmarks of a genuine apologia.*

From *Religio Laici*

I

Thus Man by his own strength to Heaven would soar:
And would not be obliged to God for more.
Vain, wretched creature, how art thou misled
To think thy Wit these God-like notions bred!
These truths are not the product of thy mind,
But dropped from Heaven, and of a nobler kind.
Revealed religion first informed thy sight,
And Reason saw not till Faith sprung the light.
Hence all thy Natural Worship takes the source:
'Tis Revelation what thou thinkst Discourse.

But if there be a Power too just and strong
To wink at crimes and bear unpunished wrong,
Look humbly upward, see his will disclose
The forfeit first, and then the fine impose,
A mulct thy poverty could never pay
Had not eternal wisdom found the way
And with celestial wealth supplied thy store;
His justice makes the fine, his mercy quits the score.
See God descending in thy human frame;
The offended, suffering in the offender's name.
All thy misdeeds to Him imputed see,
And all His righteousness devolved on thee.

From *The Hind and the Panther*

What weight of ancient witness can prevail,
If private reason hold the public scale?
But, gracious God, how well dost thou provide
For erring judgements an unerring Guide!
Thy throne is darkness in th' abyss of light,
A blaze of glory that forbids the sight;
O teach me to believe Thee thus conceal'd,
And search no farther than Thyself reveal'd;
But her alone for my Director take
Whom Thou hast promis'd never to forsake!
My thoughtless youth was wing'd with vain desires,
My manhood, long misled with wandring fires,
Follow'd false lights; and when their glimpse was gone,
My pride struck out new sparkles of her own.
Such was I, such by nature still I am,
Be Thine the glory and be mine the shame.
Good life be now my task: my doubts are done,
(What more could fright my faith, than Three in One?)
Can I believe eternal God could lie

Disguis'd in mortal mould and infancy?
That the great Maker of the world could die?
And after that, trust my imperfect sense
Which calls in question his omnipotence?
Can I my reason to my faith compel,
And shall my sight, and touch, and taste rebel?
Superior faculties are set aside,
Shall their subservient organs be my guide?
Then let the moon usurp the rule of day,
And winking tapers show the sun his way:
For what my senses can themselves perceive
I need no revelation to believe.

~

THOMAS TRAHERNE
(*ca.* 1636–1674)

Traherne's poetry is distinctive for its blend of unworldly Christian mysticism coupled with an epicurean delight in the legitimate pleasures of the body.

The Salutation

These little limbs,
These eyes and hands which here I find,
This panting heart wherewith my life begins,
Where have ye been? Behind
What curtain were ye from me hid so long?
Where was, in what abyss, my new-made tongue?

When silent I
So many thousand thousand years
Beneath the dust did in a Chaos lie,
How could I Smiles, or Tears,
Or Lips, or Hands, or Eyes, or Ears perceive?
Welcome ye treasures which I now receive.

I that so long
Was Nothing from eternity
Did little think such joys as ear and tongue
To celebrate or see;
Such sounds to hear, such hands to feel, such feet,
Such eyes and objects, on the ground to meet.

New burnished joys!
Which finest gold and pearl excel!
Such sacred treasures are the limbs of boys
In which a soul doth dwell;
Their organized joints and azure veins
More wealth include than the dead world contains.

From dust I rise
And out of Nothing now awake.
These brighter regions which salute mine eyes
    A gift from God I take.
The earth, the seas, the light, the lofty skies,
The sun and stars are mine; if these I prize.

    A stranger here
Strange things doth meet, strange glory see,
Strange treasures lodg'd in this fair world appear,
    Strange all and new to me;
But that they mine should be who Nothing was,
That strangest is of all; yet brought to pass.

From *Christian Ethicks*

For man to act as if his soul did see
The very brightness of eternity;
For man to act as if his love did burn
Above the spheres, even while it's in its urn;
For man to act even in the wilderness
As if he did those sovereign joys possess
Which do at once confirm, stir up, inflame
And perfect angels—having not the same!
It doth increase the value of his deeds;
In this a man a Seraphim exceeds.
    To act on obligations yet unknown,
To act upon rewards as yet unshown,
To keep commands whose beauty's yet unseen,
To cherish and retain a zeal between
Sleeping and waking, shows a constant care;
And that a deeper love, a love so rare
That no eye-service may with it compare.
    The angels, who are faithful while they view
His glory, know not what themselves would do,
Were they in our estate! A dimmer light

Perhaps would make them err as well as we;
And in the coldness of a darker night
Forgetful and lukewarm themselves might be.
Our very rust shall cover us with gold,
Or dust shall sparkle while their eyes behold
The glory springing from a feeble state,
Where mere belief doth, if not conquer fate,
Surmount, and pass what it doth antedate.

~

THOMAS KEN
(1637–1711)

In 1679 Thomas Ken was appointed by Charles II chaplain to Princess Mary, wife of William of Orange. Having offended William, he returned to England and became a royal chaplain. In 1685 he was consecrated Bishop of Bath and Wells but was deprived of his bishopric in 1691 because of his refusal to take the oath to William at the Revolution. Today he is probably best known for his popular morning and evening hymns, 'Awake, my soul' and 'Glory to Thee, my God, this night', the latter of which is published here.

Glory to Thee, My God, This Night

Glory to thee, my God, this night
For all the blessings of the light;
Keep me, O keep me, King of kings,
Beneath thy own almighty wings.

Forgive me Lord, for thy dear Son,
The ill that I this day have done,
That with the world, myself, and thee
I, ere I sleep, at peace may be.

Teach me to live, that I may dread
The grave as little as my bed;
Teach me to die, that so I may
Rise glorious at the awful day.

O may my soul on thee repose,
And with sweet sleep mine eyelids close,
Sleep that may me more vigorous make
To serve my God when I awake.

When in the night I sleepless lie,
My soul with heavenly thoughts supply;
Let no ill dreams disturb my rest,
No powers of darkness me molest.

Praise God, from whom all blessings flow,
Praise him, all creatures here below,
Praise him above, ye heavenly host,
Praise Father, Son, and Holy Ghost.

JEANNE MARIE DE LA MOTTE-GUYON
(1648–1717)

Born into a very pious family, Jeanne Marie de la Bouvier was a sickly child who received little formal education. At sixteen she married Jacques Guyon, twenty-two years her senior. Twelve years later she lost her husband and two of her children in quick succession. Still only twenty-eight years old, but a widow with three surviving children, she found that the sufferings she had experienced led her towards mysticism. For a while she was suspected of heresy and was imprisoned for seven months. Yet her reputation as a mystic began to spread throughout Europe. Her work was published in Holland in 1704 and, across the Channel, English theologians and scholars began to read her works avidly.

The Benefits of Suffering

By sufferings only can we know
    The nature of the life we live;
The temper of our souls they show,
    How true, how pure, the love we give.
To leave my love in doubt would be
No less disgrace than misery!

I welcome, then, with heart sincere,
    The cross my Saviour bids me take;
No load, no trial, is severe,
    That's borne or suffered for His sake:
And thus my sorrow shall proclaim
A love that's worthy of the name.

I Love My God

I love my God, but with no love of mine,
 For I have none to give;
I love thee, Lord; but all the love is Thine,
 For by Thy life I live.
I am as nothing, and rejoice to be
Emptied, and lost, and swallowed up in Thee.

Thou, Lord, alone, art all Thy children need,
 And there is none beside;
From Thee the streams of blessedness proceed
 In Thee the blest abide,—
Fountain of Life, and all-abounding grace,
Our source, our centre, and our dwelling-place.

~

JOSEPH ADDISON
(1672–1719)

Known principally as an essayist, Addison's ode to Creation displays his unsung talent as a poet.

Ode

The spacious firmament on high,
With all the blue ethereal sky,
And spangled heav'ns, a shining frame,
Their great original proclaim:
Th'unwearied sun, from day to day,
Does his creator's power display,
And publishes to every land
The work of an almighty hand.

Soon as the evening shades prevail,
The moon takes up the wondrous tale,
And nightly to the listening earth
Repeats the story of her birth:
Whilst all the stars that round her burn,
And all the planets, in their turn,
Confirm the tidings as they roll,
And spread the truth from pole to pole.

What though, in solemn silence, all
Move round the dark terrestrial ball?
What tho' nor real voice nor sound
Amid their radiant orbs be found?
In reason's ear they all rejoice,
And utter forth a glorious voice,
For ever singing, as they shine,
'The hand that made us is divine.'

CHARLES WESLEY
(1707–1788)

Often overshadowed by his more famous brother, Charles Wesley is best known as a prolific writer of hymns. By the time of his death he had written more than 5,500, including the ever popular 'Jesu, Lover of my soul' and 'Love divine, all loves excelling'.

Lines Written during His Courtship

Christ, my Life, my Only Treasure,
    Thou alone
    Mould thine own,
  After thy Good pleasure.

Thou, who paidst my Price, direct me!
    Thine I am,
    Holy Lamb,
  Save, and always save me.

Order Thou my whole Condition,
    Choose my State,
    Fix my Fate
  By thy wise Decision.

From all Earthly Expectation
    Set me free,
    Seize for Thee
  All my Strength of Passion.

Into absolute Subjection
    Be it brought,
    Every Thought,
  Every fond Affection.

That which most my Soul requires
    For thy sake
    Hold it back
  Purge my Best Desires.

Keep from me thy loveliest Creature,
    Till I prove
    Jesus' Love
  Infinitely sweeter;

Till with purest Passion panting
    Cries my Heart
    'Where Thou art
  Nothing more is wanting.'

Blest with thine Abiding Spirit,
    Fully blest
    Now I rest,
  All in Thee inherit.

Heaven is now with Jesus given;
    Christ in me,
    Thou shalt be
  Mine Eternal Heaven.

On the Death of His Son

Dead! dead! the Child I lov'd so well!
  Transported to the world above!
I need no more my heart conceal.
  I never dar'd indulge my love:
But may I not indulge my grief,
And seek in tears a sad relief?

Mine earthly happiness is fled,
  His mother's joy, his father's hope,
(O had I dy'd in Isaac's stead!)
  He should have lived, my age's prop.
He should have clos'd his father's eyes,
And follow'd me to paradise.

But hath not heaven, who first bestowed,
    A right to take his gifts away?
I bow me to the sovereign God,
    Who snatched him from the evil day!
Yet nature will repeat her moan,
And fondly cry, 'My son, my son!'

Turn from him, turn, officious thought!
    Officious thought presents again
The thousand little acts he wrought,
    Which wound my heart with soothing pain:
His looks, his winning gestures rise,
His waving hands, and laughing eyes!

Those waving hands no more shall move.
    Those laughing eyes shall smile no more:
He cannot now engage our love.
    With sweet insinuating power
Our weak unguarded hearts insnare,
And rival his Creator there.

From us, as we from him, secure,
    Caught to his heavenly Father's breast,
He waits, till we the bliss insure,
    From all these stormy sorrows rest,
And see him with our Angel stand,
To waft, and welcome us to land.

∼

JOHN NEWTON
(1725–1807)

John Newton, like Charles Wesley, is best known as a writer of hymns.
The following is one of the most popular.

How Sweet the Name of Jesus Sounds

How sweet the Name of Jesus sounds
    In a believer's ear!
It soothes his sorrows, heals his wounds,
    And drives away his fear!

It makes the wounded spirit whole
    And calms the troubled breast:
'Tis manna to the hungry soul,
    And to the weary, rest.

Dear Name! the rock on which I build,
    My shield and hiding-place,
My never-failing treasury, fill'd
    With boundless stores of grace,—

By Thee my prayers acceptance gain,
    Although with sin defiled;
Satan accuses me in vain,
    And I am own'd a Child.

Weak is the effort of my heart,
    And cold my warmest thought;
But, when I see Thee as Thou art,
    I'll praise Thee as I ought.

Till then, I would Thy love proclaim
    With every fleeting breath;
And may the music of Thy Name
    Refresh my soul in death!

WILLIAM COWPER
(1731–1800)

John Newton was to exert a considerable influence upon William Cowper after the latter had moved to Olney in Buckinghamshire where Newton was curate. It is often suggested that this influence was harmful to Cowper's delicate mental health but their collaboration on the Olney Hymns *produced a wealth of hymns still popular today.*

Walking with God

Oh! for a closer walk with God,
    A calm and heavenly frame;
A light to shine upon the road
    That leads me to the Lamb!

Where is the blessedness I knew
    When first I saw the Lord?
Where is the soul-refreshing view
    Of Jesus and his word?

What peaceful hours I once enjoyed!
    How sweet their memory still!
But they have left an aching void
    The world can never fill.

Return, O holy Dove, return,
    Sweet messenger of rest;
I hate the sins that made thee mourn,
    And drove thee from my breast.

The dearest idol I have known,
    Whate'er that idol be,
Help me to tear it from thy throne,
    And worship only Thee.

So shall my walk be close with God,
    Calm and serene my frame;
So purer light shall mark the road
    That leads me to the Lamb.

Exhortation to Prayer

What various hindrances we meet
In coming to a mercy-seat!
Yet who that knows the worth of pray'r
But wishes to be often there?

Pray'r makes the dark'ned cloud withdraw,
Pray'r climbs the ladder Jacob saw,
Gives exercise to faith and love,
Brings ev'ry blessing from above.

Restraining pray'r, we cease to fight;
Pray'r makes the Christian's armour bright;
And Satan trembles, when he sees
The weakest saint upon his knees.

While Moses stood with arms spread wide,
Success was found on Israel's side;
But when thro' weakness they fail'd,
That moment Amalek prevail'd.

Have you no words? Ah, think again!
Words flow apace when you complain
And fill your fellow-creature's ear
With the sad tale of all your care.

Were half the breath thus vainly spent
To heav'n in supplication sent,
Your cheerful song would oft'ner be:
'Hear what the Lord has done for me!'

WILLIAM BLAKE
(1757–1827)

Along with Wordsworth and Coleridge, William Blake was a leading light in the Romantic reaction against the rationalism and materialism of the Enlightenment. Unlike Wordsworth and Coleridge, his relationship with traditional Christianity remained eccentrically and eclectically heterodox. Although much of his poetry can be considered Christian only in the loosest sense of the word, it often contains elements of mist and mysticism, entwined with Christian imagery and a condemnation of 'satanic' industrialism, with which many Christians will sympathise.

From Milton: Jerusalem

And did those feet in ancient time
Walk upon England's mountains green?
And was the holy Lamb of God
On England's pleasant pastures seen?

And did the Countenance Divine
Shine forth upon our clouded hills?
And was Jerusalem builded here
Among these dark Satanic Mills?

Bring me my Bow of burning gold:
Bring me my Arrows of desire:
Bring me my Spear: O clouds unfold!
Bring me my Chariot of fire.

I will not cease from Mental Fight,
Nor shall my Sword sleep in my hand
Till we have built Jerusalem
In England's green & pleasant Land.

SAMUEL TAYLOR COLERIDGE
(1772–1834)

The son of a vicar at Ottery St Mary in Devon, Coleridge rebelled against his Christian upbringing and dabbled in revolutionary politics, decadence and opium before returning to religion. Thereafter, his resolute defence of orthodoxy, rooted in a firm grasp of philosophy, made him a champion of traditional Christian teaching. The 'Epitaph', the last of his verses published below, was written on 9 November 1833, only months before his death.

Hymn Before Sun-Rise in the Vale of Chamouni

Hast thou a charm to stay the morning-star
In his steep course? So long he seems to pause
On thy bald awful head, O sovran BLANC!
The Arve and Arveiron at thy base
Rave ceaselessly; but thou, most awful Form!
Risest from forth thy silent sea of pines,
How silently! Around thee and above
Deep is the air and dark, substantial, black,
An ebon mass: methinks thou piercest it,
As with a wedge! But when I look again,
It is thine own calm home, thy crystal shrine,
Thy habitation from eternity!
O dread and silent Mount! I gazed upon thee,
Till thou, still present to the bodily sense,
Didst vanish from my thought: entranced in prayer
I worshipped the Invisible alone.

Yet, like some sweet beguiling melody,
So sweet, we know not we are listening to it,
Thou, the meanwhile, wast blending with my Thought,
Yea, with my Life and Life's own secret joy:

Till the dilating Soul, enrapt, transfused,
Into the mighty vision passing—there
As in her natural form, swelled vast to Heaven!

Awake, my soul! not only passive praise
Thou owest! not alone these swelling tears,
Mute thanks and secret ecstasy! Awake,
Voice of sweet song! Awake, my heart, awake!
Green vales and icy cliffs, all join my hymn.

Thou first and chief, sole sovereign of the Vale!
O struggling with the darkness all the night,
And visited all night by troops of stars,
Or when they climb the sky or when they sink:
Companion of the morning-star at dawn,
Thyself Earth's rosy star, and of the dawn
Co-herald: wake, O wake, and utter praise!
Who sank thy sunless pillars deep in Earth?
Who filled thy countenance with rosy light?
Who made thee parent of perpetual streams?

And you, ye five wild torrents fiercely glad!
Who called you forth from night and utter death,
From dark and icy caverns called you forth,
Down those precipitous, black, jaggèd rocks,
For ever shattered and the same for ever?
Who gave you your invulnerable life,
Your strength, your speed, your fury, and your joy,
Unceasing thunder and eternal foam?
And who commanded (and the silence came),
Here let the billows stiffen, and have rest?

Ye Ice-falls! ye that from the mountain's brow
Adown enormous ravines slope amain—
Torrents, methinks, that heard a mighty voice,
And stopped at once amid their maddest plunge!
Motionless torrents! silent cataracts!
Who made you glorious as the Gates of Heaven

Beneath the keen full moon? Who bade the sun
Clothe you with rainbows? Who, with living flowers
Of loveliest blue, spread garlands at your feet?—
GOD! let the torrents, like a shout of nations,
Answer! and let the ice-plains echo, GOD!
GOD! sing ye meadow-streams with gladsome voice!
Ye pine-groves, with your soft and soul-like sounds!
And they too have a voice, yon piles of snow,
And in their perilous fall shall thunder, GOD!

Ye living flowers that skirt the eternal frost!
Ye wild goats sporting round the eagle's nest!
Ye eagles, play-mates of the mountain-storm!
Ye lightnings, the dread arrows of the clouds!
Ye signs and wonders of the element!
Utter forth God, and fill the hills with praise!

Thou too, hoar Mount! with thy sky-pointing peaks,
Oft from whose feet the avalanche, unheard,
Shoots downward, glittering through the pure serene
Into the depth of clouds, that veil thy breast—
Thou too again, stupendous Mountain! thou
That as I raise my head, awhile bowed low
In adoration, upward from thy base
Slow travelling, with dim eyes suffused with tears,
Solemnly seemest, like a vapoury cloud,
To rise before me—Rise, O ever rise,
Rise like a cloud of incense from the Earth!
Thou kingly Spirit throned among the hills,
Thou dread ambassador from Earth to Heaven,
Great Hierarch! tell thou the silent sky,
And tell the stars, and tell yon rising sun
Earth, with her thousand voices, praises God.

The Virgin's Cradle-Hymn

(Copied from a print of the Virgin
in a Catholic village in Germany)

Dormi, Jesu! Mater ridet
Quae tam dulcem somnum videt,
   Dormi, Jesu! blandule!
Si non dormis, Mater plorat,
Inter fila cantans orat,
   Blande, veni, somnule.

Sleep, sweet babe! My cares beguiling:
Mother sits beside thee smiling;
   Sleep, my darling, tenderly!
If thou sleep not, mother mourneth,
Singing as her wheel she turneth:
   Come, soft slumber, balmily!

A Hymn

My Maker! of thy power the trace
In every creature's form and face
   The wond'ring soul surveys:
Thy wisdom, infinite above
Seraphic thought, a Father's love
   As infinite displays!
From all that meets or eye or ear,
There falls a genial holy fear
Which, like the heavy dew of morn
Refreshes while it bows the heart forlorn!

Great God! thy works how wondrous fair!
Yet sinful man didst thou declare
   The whole Earth's voice and mind!
Lord, ev'n as Thou all-present art,
O may we still with heedful heart
   Thy presence know and find!

Then, come, what will, of weal or woe,
Joy's bosom-spring shall steady flow;
For though 'tis Heaven Thyself to see,
Where but thy Shadow falls, Grief cannot be!

To Nature

It may indeed be phantasy when I
Essay to draw from all created things
Deep, heartfelt, inward joy that closely clings;
And trace in leaves and flowers that round me lie
Lessons of love and earnest piety.
So let it be; and if the wide world rings
In mock of this belief, it brings
Nor fear, nor grief, nor vain perplexity.
So will I build my altar in the fields,
And the blue sky my fretted dome shall be,
And the sweet fragrance that the wild flower yields
Shall be the incense I will yield to Thee,
Thee only God! and thou shalt not despise
Even me, the priest of this poor sacrifice.

My Baptismal Birthday

God's child in Christ adopted,—Christ my all,—
What that earth boasts were not lost cheaply, rather
Than forfeit that blest name, by which I call
The Holy One, the Almighty God, my Father? —
Father! in Christ we live, and Christ in Thee—
Eternal Thou, and everlasting we.
The heir of heaven, henceforth I fear not death:
In Christ I live! in Christ I draw the breath
Of the true life!—Let, then, earth, sea, and sky
Make war against me! On my front I show
Their mighty Master's seal. In vain they try
To end my life, that can but end its woe.—

Is that a deathbed where a Christian lies?
Yes! but not his—'tis Death itself that dies.

Epitaph

Stop, Christian Passer-by! —Stop, child of God,
And read with gentle breast. Beneath this sod
A poet lies, or that which one seem'd he.—
Oh! lift one thought in prayer for S.T.C.;
That he who many a year with toil of breath
Found death in life, may here find life in death!
Mercy for praise—to be forgiven for fame
He ask'd, and hoped, through Christ. Do thou the same!

JOHN HENRY NEWMAN
(1801–1890)

*Perhaps Newman can be considered the founding father of the Catholic
literary revival in England. Ordained in the Anglican Church in 1824,
he soon became embroiled in the divisions between the Anglo-Catholic
and Evangelical parties in the Church of England. Siding solidly with
the Anglo-Catholics, Newman rose to fame and prominence as a lead-
ing member of the Tractarian movement. His reception into the Roman
Catholic Church in 1845 caused great controversy. He explained his
reasons for conversion in the autobiographical* Apologia Pro Vita Sua
and in the semi-autobiographical novel, Loss and Gain. *Although he is
considered primarily as a theologian, these two works, together with his
collected poems, ensure his place among the* illustrissimi *of Victorian
writers.*

From *The Dream of Gerontius*

GERONTIUS

Jesu, Maria—I am near to death,
   And Thou art calling me; I know it now.
Not by the token of this faltering breath,
   This chill at heart, this dampness on my brow,—
(Jesu, have mercy! Mary, pray for me!)
   'Tis this new feeling, never felt before,
(Be with me, Lord, in my extremity!)
   That I am going, that I am no more.
'Tis this strange innermost abandonment,
   (Lover of souls! great God! I look to Thee,)
This emptying out of each constituent
   And natural force, by which I came to be.
Pray for me, O my friends; a visitant
   Is knocking his dire summons at my door,

The like of whom, to scare me and to daunt,
    Has never, never come to me before;
'Tis death,—O loving friends, your prayers!—'tis he! . . .

* * *

GERONTIUS

Rouse thee, my fainting soul, and play the man;
    And through such waning span
Of life and thought as still has to be trod,
    Prepare to meet thy God.
And while the storm of the bewilderment
    Is for a season spent,
And, ere afresh the ruin on me fall,
    Use well the interval.

ASSISTANTS

Be merciful, be gracious; spare him, Lord.
Be merciful, be gracious; Lord, deliver him.
From the sins that are past;
    From Thy frown and Thine ire;
        From the perils of dying;
        From any complying
        With sin, or denying
        His God, or relying
On self, at the last;
    From the nethermost fire;
From all that is evil;
From power of the devil;
Thy servant deliver,
For once and for ever.

By Thy birth, and by Thy Cross,
Rescue him from endless loss;
By Thy death and burial,
Save him from a final fall;

By Thy rising from the tomb,
   By Thy mounting up above,
   By the Spirit's gracious love,
Save him in the day of doom.

GERONTIUS

Sanctus fortis, Sanctus Deus,
   De profundis oro te,
Miserere, Judex meus,
   Parce mihi, Domine.
Firmly I believe and truly
   God is Three, and God is One;
And I next acknowledge duly
   Manhood taken by the Son.
And I trust and hope most fully
   In that manhood crucified;
And each thought and deed unruly
   Do to death, as He has died.
Simply to His grace and wholly
   Light and life and strength belong,
And I love, supremely, solely,
   Him the holy, Him the strong.
Sanctus fortis, Sanctus Deus,
   De profundis oro te,
Miserere, Judex meus,
   Parce mihi, Domine.
And I hold in veneration,
   For the love of Him alone,
Holy Church, as His creation,
   And her teachings, as His own.
And I take with joy whatever
   Now besets me, pain or fear,
And with a strong will I sever
   All the ties which bind me here.

Adoration aye be given,
    With and through the angelic host,
To the God of earth and heaven,
    Father, Son and Holy Ghost.
Sanctus fortis, Sanctus Deus,
    De profundis oro te,
Miserere, Judex meus,
    Mortis in discrimine.

* * *

FIFTH CHOIR OF ANGELICALS

Praise to the Holiest in the height,
    And in the depth be praise:
In all His words most wonderful;
    Most sure in all His ways!

O loving wisdom of our God!
    When all was sin and shame,
A second Adam to the fight
    And to the rescue came.

O wisest love! that flesh and blood
    Which did in Adam fail,
Should strive afresh against their foe,
    Should strive and should prevail;

And that a higher gift than grace
    Should flesh and blood refine,
God's Presence and His very Self,
    And Essence all-divine.

* * *

ANGEL

Softly and gently, dearly-ransom'd soul,
    In my most loving arms I now enfold thee,

And, o'er the penal waters, as they roll,
  I poise thee, and I lower thee, and hold thee

And carefully I dip thee in the lake,
  And thou, without a sob or a resistance,
Dost through the flood thy rapid passage take,
  Sinking deep, deeper, into the dim distance.

Angels, to whom the willing task is given,
  Shall tend, and nurse, and lull thee, as thou liest;
And Masses on the earth, and prayers in heaven,
  Shall aid thee at the Throne of the Most Highest.

Farewell, but not for ever! brother dear,
  Be brave and patient on thy bed of sorrow;
Swiftly shall pass thy night of trial here,
  And I will come and wake thee on the morrow.

The Sign of the Cross

Whene'er across this sinful flesh of mine
  I draw the Holy Sign,
All good thoughts stir within me, and renew
  Their slumbering strength divine;
Till there springs up a courage high and true
  To suffer and to do.

And who shall say, but hateful spirits around,
  For their brief hour unbound,
Shudder to see, and wail their overthrow?
  While on far heathen ground
Some lonely Saint hails the fresh odour, though
  Its source he cannot know.

The Pilgrim Queen
(A Song)

There sat a Lady
　　all on the ground,
Rays of the morning
　　circled her round,
Save thee, and hail to thee,
　　Gracious and Fair,
In the chill twilight
　　what wouldst thou there?

'Here I sit desolate,'
　　sweetly said she,
'Though I'm a queen,
　　and my name is Marie:
Robbers have rifled
　　my garden and store,
Foes they have stolen
　　my heir from my bower.

'They said they could keep Him
　　far better than I,
In a palace all His,
　　planted deep and raised high.
'Twas a palace of ice,
　　hard and cold as were they,
And when summer came,
　　it all melted away.

'Next would they barter Him,
　　Him the Supreme,
For the spice of the desert,
　　and gold of the stream;
And me they bid wander
　　in weeds and alone,
In this green merry land
　　which once was my own.'

I looked on that Lady,
  and out from her eyes
Came the deep glowing blue
  of Italy's skies;
And she raised up her head
  and she smiled, as a Queen
On the day of her crowning,
  so bland and serene.

'A moment,' she said,
  'and the dead shall revive;
The giants are failing,
  the Saints are alive;
I am coming to rescue
  my home and my reign,
And Peter and Philip
  are close in my train.'

Guardian Angel

My oldest friend, mine from the hour
  When first I drew my breath;
My faithful friend, that shall be mine,
  Unfailing, till my death;

Thou hast been ever at my side;
  My Maker to thy trust
Consign'd my soul, what time He framed
  The infant child of dust.

No beating heart in holy prayer,
  No faith, inform'd aright,
Gave me to Joseph's tutelage,
  Or Michael's conquering might.

Nor patron Saint, nor Mary's love,
  The dearest and the best,

Has known my being, as thou hast known,
    And blest, as thou hast blest.

Thou wast my sponsor at the font;
    And thou, each budding year,
Didst whisper elements of truth
    Into my childish ear.

And when, ere boyhood yet was gone,
    My rebel spirit fell,
Ah! thou didst see, and shudder too,
    Yet bear each deed of Hell.

And then in turn, when judgements came,
    And scared me back again,
Thy quick soft breath was near to soothe
    And hallow every pain.

Oh! who of all thy toils and cares
    Can tell the tale complete,
To place me under Mary's smile,
    And Peter's royal feet!

And thou wilt hang about my bed,
    When life is ebbing low;
Of doubt, impatience, and of gloom,
    The jealous sleepless foe.

Mine, when I stand before the Judge;
    And mine, if spared to stay
Within the golden furnace, till
    My sin is burn'd away.

And mine, O Brother of my soul,
    When my release shall come;
Thy gentle arms shall lift me then,
    Thy wings shall waft me home.

The Golden Prison

Weep not for me, when I am gone,
  Nor spend thy faithful breath
In grieving o'er the spot or hour
  Of all-enshrouding death;

Nor waste in idle praise thy love
  On deeds of head or hand,
Which live within the living Book,
  Or else are writ in sand;

But let it be thy best of prayers,
  That I may find the grace
To reach the holy house of toll,
  The frontier penance-place,—

To reach that golden palace bright,
  Where souls elect abide,
Waiting their certain call to Heaven,
  With Angels at their side;

Where hate, nor pride, nor fear torments
  The transitory guest,
But in the willing agony
  He plunges, and is blest.

And as the fainting patriarch gain'd
  His needful halt mid-way,
And then refresh'd pursued his path,
  Where up the mount it lay,

So pray, that, rescued from the storm
  Of heaven's eternal ire,
I may lie down, then rise again,
  Safe, and yet saved by fire.

For the Dead

(A Hymn)

Help, Lord, the souls which Thou hast made,
   The souls to Thee so dear,
In prison, for the debt unpaid
   Of sins committed here.

Those holy souls, they suffer on,
   Resign'd in heart and will,
Until Thy high behest is done,
   And justice has its fill.
For daily falls, for pardon'd crime,
   They joy to undergo
The shadow of Thy cross sublime,
   The remnant of Thy woe.

Help, Lord, the souls which Thou hast made,
   The souls to Thee so dear,
In prison, for the debt unpaid
   Of sins committed here.

Oh, by their patience of delay,
   Their hope amid their pain,
Their sacred zeal to burn away
   Disfigurement and stain;
Oh, by their fire of love, not less
   In keenness than the flame,
Oh, by their very helplessness,
   Oh, by Thy own great Name,

Good Jesu, help! sweet Jesu, aid
   The souls to Thee most dear,
In prison, for the debt unpaid
   Of sins committed here.

∼

ELIZABETH BARRETT BROWNING
(1806–1861)

Although Elizabeth Barrett Browning is undoubtedly one of the finest poets of the Victorian age, she is seldom considered as a specifically Christian writer. The apparent ambivalence with which she approached religious themes is evident in this verse which nonetheless comes to mystical fruition through an almost Franciscan reverence for creation.

Patience Taught by Nature

'O dreary life,' we cry, 'O dreary life!'
And still the generations of the birds
Sing through our sighing, and the flocks and herds
Serenely live while we are keeping strife
With Heaven's true purpose in us, as a knife
Against which we may struggle! ocean girds
Unslackened the dry land, savannah-swards
Unweary sweep,—hills watch, unworn; and rife
Meek leaves drop yearly from the forest-trees,
To show above the unwasted stars that pass
In their old glory. O thou God of old,
Grant me some smaller grace than comes to these!—
But so much patience as a blade of grass
Grows by, contented through the heat and cold.

JOHN GREENLEAF WHITTIER
(1807–1892)

John Greenleaf Whittier was an American Quaker, born near Haver-hill, Massachusetts, the son of a poor farmer. He became a leading abolitionist, devoting himself to the cause of emancipation, but was also renowned as a poet. In his day he was considered second only to Longfel-low. Today, he is probably most remembered for the section of his poem 'The Brewing of Soma' which has become one of the most popular hymns in the English language.

From *The Brewing of Soma*

Dear Lord and Father of mankind,
　　Forgive our foolish ways!
Reclothe us in our rightful mind,
In purer lives thy service find,
　　In deeper reverence, praise.

In simple trust like theirs who heard
　　Beside the Syrian sea
The gracious calling of the Lord,
Let us, like them, without a word,
　　Rise up and follow thee.

O Sabbath rest by Galilee!
　　O calm of hills above,
Where Jesus knelt to share with thee
The silence of eternity
　　Interpreted by love!

With that deep hush subduing all
　　Our words and works that drown
The tender whisper of thy call,
As noiseless let thy blessing fall
　　As fell thy manna down.

Drop thy still dews of quietness,
    Till all our strivings cease;
Take from our souls the strain and stress,
And let our ordered lives confess
    The beauty of thy peace.

Breathe through the heats of our desire
    Thy coolness and thy balm;
Let sense be dumb, let flesh retire;
Speak through the earthquake, wind, and fire,
    O still, small voice of calm!

~

HENRY WADSWORTH LONGFELLOW
(1807–1882)

Born in the same year as John Greenleaf Whittier, Longfellow was the most celebrated American poet of his generation. Today he is best known for poems such as Hiawatha *which display his gift of simple romantic story-telling in verse. He is less known for his translation of Dante or for this short yet charming verse which was written in honour of Italy's greatest poet.*

Dante

Oft have I seen at some cathedral door
    A labourer, pausing in the dust and heat,
    Lay down his burden, and with reverent feet
    Enter, and cross himself, and on the floor
Kneel to repeat his paternoster o'er;
    Far off the noises of the world retreat;
    The loud vociferations of the street
    Become an undistinguishable roar.
So, as I enter here from day to day,
    And leave my burden at this minster gate,
    Kneeling in prayer, and not ashamed to pray,
The tumult of the time disconsolate
    To inarticulate murmurs dies away,
    While the eternal ages watch and wait.

ALFRED, LORD TENNYSON
(1809–1892)

In 1850 Tennyson succeeded Wordsworth as poet laureate, a recognition of his increasing fame and popularity in Victorian England. For the next forty years he remained the dominant force in English poetry, his achievement being crowned with the bestowal of a peerage on him in 1884. Ironically, however, most of his best work dates from the beginning of his literary career and was included in the volume of verse published in 1842 and in the loosely connected elegies, collectively titled In Memoriam, *published in 1850. In later life Tennyson became increasingly concerned with the apparent conflict between science and the Faith, a theme which would dominate the work of many of the poets who followed him.*

From *In Memoriam*

XXVIII

The time draws near the birth of Christ:
   The moon is hid; the night is still;
   The Christmas bells from hill to hill
Answer each other in the mist.

Four voices of four hamlets round,
   From far and near, on mead and moor,
   Swell out and fail, as if a door
Were shut between me and the sound;

Each voice four changes on the wind,
   That now dilate and now decrease,
   Peace and goodwill, goodwill and peace,
Peace and goodwill, to all mankind.

This year I slept and woke with pain,
    I almost wished no more to wake,
    And that my hold on life would break
Before I heard those bells again;

But they my troubled spirit rule,
    For they controlled me when a boy;
    They bring me sorrow touched with joy,
The merry, merry bells of Yule.

XLIX

Be near me when my light is low,
    When the blood creeps, and the nerves prick
    And tingle; and the heart is sick,
And all the wheels of Being slow.

Be near me when the sensuous frame
    Is racked with pangs that conquer trust;
    And Time, a maniac scattering dust,
And Life, a Fury slinging flame.

Be near me when my faith is dry,
    And men the flies of latter spring,
    That lay their eggs, and sting and sing,
And weave their petty cells and die.

Be near me when I fade away,
    To point the term of human strife,
    And on the low dark verge of life
The twilight of eternal day.

CV

Ring out, wild bells, to the wild sky,
    The flying cloud, the frosty light:
    The year is dying in the night;
Ring out, wild bells, and let him die.

Ring out the old, ring in the new,
  Ring, happy bells, across the snow:
  The year is going, let him go;
Ring out the false, ring in the true.

Ring out the grief that saps the mind,
  For those that here we see no more;
  Ring out the feud of rich and poor,
Ring in redress to all mankind.

Ring out a slowly dying cause,
  And ancient forms of party strife;
  Ring in the nobler modes of life,
With sweeter manners, purer laws.

Ring out the want, the care, the sin,
  The faithless coldness of the times;
  Ring out, ring out my mournful rhymes,
But ring the fuller minstrel in.

Ring out false pride in place and blood,
  The civic slander and the spite;
  Ring in the love of truth and right,
Ring in the common love of good.

Ring out old shapes of foul disease;
  Ring out the narrowing lust of gold;
  Ring out the thousand wars of old,
Ring in the thousand years of peace.

Ring in the valiant man and free,
  The larger heart, the kindlier hand;
  Ring out the darkness of the land,
Ring in the Christ that is to be.

CXXIII

That which we dare invoke to bless;
  Our dearest faith; our ghastliest doubt;

He, They, One, All; within, without;
The Power in darkness whom we guess;

I found him not in world or sun,
    Or eagle's wing, or insect's eye;
    Nor through the questions men may try,
The petty cobwebs we have spun:

If e'er when faith had fallen asleep,
    I heard a voice 'believe no more'
    And heard an ever-breaking shore
That tumbled in the Godless deep;

A warmth within the breast would melt
    The freezing reason's colder part,
    And like a man in wrath the heart
Stood up and answered 'I have felt.'

No, like a child in doubt and fear:
    But that blind clamour made me wise;
    Then was I as a child that cries,
But, crying, knows his father near;

And what I am beheld again
    What is, and no man understands;
    And out of darkness came the hands
That reach through nature, moulding men.

∼

St Agnes' Eve

Deep on the convent-roof the snows
    Are sparkling to the moon:
My breath to heaven like vapour goes:
    May my soul follow soon!

The shadows of the convent-towers
    Slant down the snowy sward,
Still creeping with the creeping hours
    That lead me to the Lord:
Make Thou my spirit pure and clear
    As are the frosty skies,
Or this first snowdrop of the year
    That in my bosom lies.

As these white robes are soil'd and dark,
    To yonder shining ground;
As this pale taper's earthly spark,
    To yonder argent round;
So shows my soul before the Lamb,
    My spirit before Thee;
So in mine earthly house I am,
    To that I hope to be.
Break up the heavens, O Lord! and far,
    Thro' all yon starlight keen,
Draw me, thy bride, a glittering star,
    In raiment white and clean.

He lifts me to the golden doors;
    The flashes come and go;
All heaven bursts her starry floors,
    And strows her lights below,
And deepens on and up! the gates
    Roll back, and far within
For me the Heavenly Bridegroom waits,
    To make me pure of sin.
The sabbaths of Eternity,
    One sabbath deep and wide—
A light upon the shining sea—
    The Bridegroom with his bride!

JONES VERY
(1813–1880)

Jones Very, an American mystic who was born and died at Salem, Massachusetts, is best known for the mystical sonnets which were published in his Essays and Poems *in 1839.*

The Created

There is naught for thee by thy haste to gain;
'Tis not the swift with Me that win the race;
Through long endurance of delaying pain,
Thine opened eye shall see thy Father's face;
Nor here nor there, where now thy feet would turn,
Thou wilt find Him who ever seeks for thee;
But let obedience quench desires that burn,
And where thou art, thy Father, too, will be.
Behold! as day by day the spirit grows,
Thou see'st by inward light things hid before;
Till what God is, thyself, his image shows;
And thou dost wear the robe that first thou wore,
When bright with radiance from his forming hand,
He saw thee Lord of all his creatures stand.

∽

JOHN MASON NEALE
(1818–1866)

From 1846 J. M. Neale was warden of Sackville College, East Grinstead, where, as a member of the Anglo-Catholic wing of the Church of England, he was inhibited by his bishop from 1849 until 1863. He wrote many books on Church history but is most remembered for his hymns.

Oh, Give Us Back the Days of Old

Oh, give us back the days of old! oh! give me back an hour!
To make us feel that Holy Church o'er death hath might and
    power.
Take hence the heathen trappings, take hence the Pagan show,
The misery, the heartlessness, the unbelief of woe:
The nodding plumes, the painted staves, the mutes in black
    array,
That get their hard-won earnings by so much grief per day:
The steeds and scarves and crowds that gaze with half-suspended
    breath
As if, of all things terrible, most terrible was death:
And let us know to what we go, and wherefore we must weep,
Or o'er the Christian's hopeful rest, or everlasting sleep.
Lay in the dead man's hand the Cross—the Cross upon his
    breast
Because beneath the shadow of the Cross he went to rest:
And let the Cross go on before—the Crucified was first
To go before the people and their chains of death to burst;
And be the widow's heart made glad with charitable dole,
And pray with calm, yet earnest, faith for the departed soul.
And be the *De Profundis* said for one of Christ's own fold,
And—for a prisoner is set free—the bells be rung not tolled.

When face to face we stand with death, thus Holy Church
 records,
He is our slave, and we, through Her, his masters and his lords.
Deck the High Altar for the Mass! Let tapers guard the hearse!
For Christ, the Light that lighteneth all, to blessing turns our
 curse,
And be Nicea's Creed intoned and be the Gospel read,
In calm, low voice, for preaching can profit not the dead.
Then forth with banner, cross, and psalm, and chant, and hymn
 and prayer,
And look not on the coffin—for our brother is not there;
His soul, we trust assuredly, is safe in Abraham's breast,
And mid Christ's many faithful, his body shall have rest.
When earth its cares and turmoils, and many sorrows cease—
By all Thy woes, by all Thy joys, Lord Jesus grant them peace.

~

COVENTRY PATMORE
(1823–1896)

Patmore was, and remains, a controversial poet. His finest poetry, which followed the death of his first wife in 1862 and his conversion to Roman Catholicism two years later, is rooted in a mystical biblical eroticism which offended fellow converts Newman and Hopkins. Patmore's erotic mysticism was most evident in The Unknown Eros, *a book of verse published in 1877. Four of the odes which comprise this volume were explicitly about his dead wife and his motherless children, one of which, 'The Toys', is reproduced below. Although Patmore's erotic language continues to offend, many others share Sir Herbert Read's judgment that much of his verse represents 'true poetry of the rarest and perhaps highest kind'.*

The Toys

My little Son, who look'd from thoughtful eyes
And moved and spoke in quiet grown-up wise,
Having my law the seventh time disobey'd,
I struck him, and dismiss'd
With hard words and unkiss'd,
—His Mother, who was patient, being dead.
Then, fearing lest his grief should hinder sleep,
I visited his bed,
But found him slumbering deep,
With darken'd eyelids, and their lashes yet
From his late sobbing wet.
And I, with moan,
Kissing away his tears, left others of my own;
For, on a table drawn beside his head,
He had put, within his reach,

A box of counters and a red-vein'd stone,
A piece of glass abraded by the beach.
And six or seven shells,
A bottle with bluebells,
And two French copper coins, ranged there with careful art,
To comfort his sad heart.
So when that night I pray'd
To God, I wept, and said:
Ah, when at last we lie with tranced breath,
Not vexing Thee in death,
And Thou rememberest of what toys
We made our joys,
How weakly understood
Thy great commanded good,
Then, fatherly not less
Than I whom Thou hast moulded from the clay,
Thou'lt leave Thy wrath, and say,
'I will be sorry for their childishness.'

Magna Est Veritas

Here, in this little Bay,
Full of tumultuous life and great repose,
Where, twice a day,
The purposeless, glad ocean comes and goes,
Under high cliffs, and far from the huge town,
I sit me down.
For want of me the world's course will not fail;
When all its work is done, the lie shall rot;
The truth is great, and shall prevail,
When none cares whether it prevail or not.

GEORGE MACDONALD
(1824–1905)

George Macdonald's books for children exerted a considerable influence on later generations of writers. G. K. Chesterton, C. S. Lewis and J. R. R. Tolkien were among those who owed a debt of gratitude to the mysticism which permeates his children's fiction. By comparison, Macdonald's poetry is now largely forgotten.

That Holy Thing

They all were looking for a king
  To slay their foes and lift them high:
Thou cam'st, a little baby thing
  That made a woman cry.

O Son of Man, to right my lot
  Naught but Thy presence can avail;
Yet on the road Thy wheels are not,
  Nor on the sea Thy sail!

My how or when Thou wilt not heed,
  But come down Thine own secret stair,
That Thou mayst answer all my need—
  Yea, every bygone prayer.

From *An Old Story*

Babe and mother, coming mage,
  Shepherd, ass, and cow!
Angels watching the new age,
  Time's intensest Now!
Heaven down-brooding, Earth upstraining,
  Far ends closing in!
Sure the eternal tide is gaining
  On the strand of sin!

From *Diary of an Old Soul*

(31 January)

O Lord, I have been talking to the people;
Thought's wheels have round me whirled a fiery zone
And the recoil of my word's airy ripple
My heart unheedful has puffed up and blown.
Therefore I cast myself before thee prone:
Lay cool hands on my burning brain and press
From my weak heart the swelling emptiness.

(16 May)

I would go near thee—but I cannot press
Into thy presence—it helps not to presume.
Thy doors are deeds.

(26 May)

My prayers, my God, flow from what I am not;
I think thy answers make me what I am.
Like weary waves thought follows upon thought,
But the still depth beneath is all thine own,
And there thou mov'st in paths to us unknown.
Out of strange strife thy peace is strangely wrought;
If the lion in us pray—thou answerest the lamb.

(16 July)

The house is not for me—it is for Him.
His royal thoughts require many a stair,
Many a tower, many an outlook fair
Of which I have no thought.

(7 August)

In holy things may be unholy greed.
Thou giv'st a glimpse of many a lovely thing
Not to be stored for use in any mind,
But only for the present spiritual need.

The holiest bread, if hoarded, soon will breed
The mammon-moth, the having-pride . . .

(10 October)

With every morn my life afresh must break
The crust of self, gathered about me fresh.

(9 November)

Only no word of mine must ever foster
The self that in a brother's bosom gnaws;
I may not fondle failing, nor the boaster
Encourage with the breath of my applause.

Mary Magdalene

With wandering eyes and aimless zeal,
    She hither, thither, goes;
Her speech, her motions, all reveal
    A mind without repose.

She climbs the hills, she haunts the sea,
    By madness tortured, driven;
One hour's forgetfulness would be
    A gift from very heaven!

She slumbers into new distress;
    The night is worse than day:
Exulting in her helplessness;
    Hell's dogs yet louder bay.

The demons blast her to and fro;
    She has not quiet place,
Enough a woman still, to know
    A haunting dim disgrace.

A human touch! a pang of death!
    And in a low delight

Thou liest, waiting for new breath,
    For morning out of night.

Thou risest up: the earth is fair,
    The wind is cool; thou art free!
Is it a dream of hell's despair
    Dissolves in ecstasy?

That man did touch thee! Eyes divine
    Make sunrise in thy soul;
Thou seest love in order shine:—
    His health hath made thee whole!

Thou, sharing in the awful doom,
    Didst help thy Lord to die;
Then, weeping o'er his empty tomb,
    Didst hear him *Mary* cry.

He stands in haste; he cannot stop;
    Home to his God he fares:
'Go tell my brothers I go up
    To my Father, mine and theirs.'

Run, Mary! lift thy heavenly voice;
    Cry, cry, and heed not how;
Make all the new-risen world rejoice—
    Its first apostle thou!

What if old tales of thee have lied,
    Or truth have told, thou art
All-safe with him, whate'er betide
    Dwell'st with him in God's heart!

∿

THOMAS EDWARD BROWN
(1830–1897)

My Garden

A garden is a lovesome thing, God wot!
  Rose plot,
  Fringed pool,
Fern'd grot—
  The veriest school
  Of peace; and yet the fool
Contends that God is not—
Not God! in gardens! when the eve is cool?
  Nay, but I have a sign;
  'Tis very sure God walks in mine.

~

CHRISTINA ROSSETTI
(1830–1894)

Christina Rossetti was descended from Italians on both sides of her family. Her father, Gabrielle Rossetti, was an exiled political radical who had come to England in 1824. Her mother, Frances Polidori, was committed to Anglo-Catholicism, a faith to which Christina herself subscribed throughout her life. Along with her two brothers, Dante Gabriel and William Michael, she was involved in the pre-Raphaelite Brotherhood, whose expressed object was to resist the conventions of modern art by a return to pre-Renaissance art forms involving vivid colour and detail. Her verse was an expression of this pre-Raphaelite spirit.

A Christmas Carol

In the bleak mid-winter,
  Frosty wind made moan,
Earth stood hard as iron,
  Water like a stone;
Snow had fallen, snow on snow,
  Snow on snow,
In the bleak mid-winter
  Long ago.

Our God, Heaven cannot hold Him
  Nor earth sustain;
Heaven and earth shall flee away
  When He comes to reign:
In the bleak mid-winter
  A stable-place sufficed
The Lord God Almighty
  Jesus Christ.

Enough for Him whom cherubim
  Worship night and day,

A breastful of milk
    And a mangerful of hay;
Enough for Him whom angels
    Fall down before,
The ox and ass and camel
    Which adore.

Angels and archangels
    May have gathered there,
Cherubim and seraphim
    Thronged the air,
But only His mother
    In her maiden bliss
Worshipped the Beloved
    With a kiss.

What can I give Him,
    Poor as I am?
If I were a shepherd
    I would bring a lamb,
If I were a wise man
    I would do my part—
Yet what I can, I give Him,
    Give my heart.

St Peter

St Peter once: 'Lord, dost Thou wash my feet?'—
    Much more I say: Lord, dost Thou stand and knock
    At my closed heart more rugged than a rock,
Bolted and barred, for Thy soft touch unmeet,
Nor garnished nor in any wise made sweet?
    Owls roost within and dancing satyrs mock.
    Lord, I have heard the crowing of the cock
And have not wept: ah, Lord, thou knowest it.
Yet still I hear Thee knocking, still I hear:
    'Open to Me, look on Me eye to eye,

That I may wring your heart and make it whole;
And teach thee love because I hold thee dear
   And sup with thee in gladness soul with soul,
And sup with thee in glory by and by.'

Mary Magdalene

She came in deep repentance,
   And knelt down at his feet
Who can change the sorrow into joy,
   The bitter into sweet.

She had cast away her jewels
   And her rich attire,
And her breast was filled with a holy shame,
   And her heart with a holy fire.

Her tears were more precious
   Than her precious pearls—
Her tears that fell upon His feet
   As she wiped them with her curls.

Her youth and her beauty
   Were budding to their prime;
But she wept for the great transgression,
   The sin of other time.

Trembling betwixt hope and fear,
   She sought the King of Heaven,
Forsook the evil of her ways,
   Loved much, and was forgiven.

~

Are Ye Not Much Better Than They?

The twig sprouteth,
The moth outeth,
The plant springeth,
The bird singeth:
Tho' little we sing today
Yet are we better than they;
Tho' growing with scarce a showing,
Yet, please God, we are growing.

The twig teacheth,
The moth preacheth,
The plant vaunteth,
The bird chanteth,
God's mercy overflowing,
Merciful past man's knowing.
Please God to keep us growing
Till the awful day of mowing.

St Elizabeth of Hungary

When if ever life is sweet,
   Save in heart in all a child,
   A fair virgin undefiled,
Knelt she at her Saviour's feet:
While she laid her royal crown,
   Thinking it too mean a thing
   For a solemn offering,
Careless on the cushions down.

Fair she was as any rose,
   But more pale than lilies white:
Her eyes full of deep repose
   Seemed to see beyond our sight.
Hush, she is a holy thing:
   Hush, her soul is in her eyes,
   Seeking far in Paradise
For her Light, her Love, her King.

The Voice of My Beloved

Once I ached for thy dear sake:
Wilt thou cause Me now to ache?
Once I bled for thee in pain:
Wilt thou rend My Heart again?
Crown of thorns and shameful tree.
Bitter death I bore for thee,
Bore My Cross to carry thee,
And wilt thou have nought of Me?

~

EMILY DICKINSON
(1830–1886)

Born in the same year as Christina Rossetti but on the other side of the Atlantic, Emily Dickinson was the other great woman writer of religious verse in the Victorian era. A solitary mystic by inclination she withdrew from all social contacts at the age of twenty-three, living a secluded life at Amherst, Massachusetts. For the next third of a century she wrote in secret over a thousand poems of widely varying quality, all but one or two of which remained unpublished until after her death.

'Bring Me the Sunset in a Cup'

Bring me the sunset in a cup,
Reckon the morning's flagons up
And say how many dew,
Tell me how far the morning leaps,
Tell me what time the weaver sleeps
Who spun the breadths of blue.

Write me how many notes there be
In the new robin's exstasy
Among astonished boughs,
How many trips the tortoise makes,
How many cups the bee partakes,
The debauchee of dews.

Also, who laid the rainbow's piers,
Also, who leads the docile spheres
By withes of supple blue?
Whose fingers string the stalactite,
Who counts the wampum of the night
To see that none is ude?

Who built this little alban house
And shut the windows down so close
My spirit cannot see?
Who'll let me out some gala day
With implements to fly away,
Passing pomposity?

'To Learn the Transport by the Pain'

To learn the transport by the pain
As blind men learn the sun,
To die of thirst suspecting
That brooks in meadows run,

To stay the homesick, homesick feet
Upon a foreign shore,
Haunted by native lands the while,
And blue, beloved air—

This is the sov'reign anguish,
This the signal woe.
These are the patient laureates
Whose voices, trained below,

Ascend in ceaseless carol,
Inaudible indeed
To us, the duller scholars
Of the mysterious bard.

'I Should Have Been Too Glad'

I should have been too glad, I see,
Too lifted for the scant degree
Of life's penurious round;
My little circuit would have shamed
This new circumference, have blamed
The homelier time behind.

I should have been too saved, I see,
Too rescued; fear too dim to me
That I could spell the prayer
I knew so perfectly yesterday,
That scalding one, 'Sabachthani',
Recited fluent here.

Earth would have been too much, I see,
And Heaven not enough for me.
I should have had the joy
Without the fear to justify,
The palm without the Calvary.
So, Saviour, crucify.

Defeat whets victory, they say.
The reefs in old Gethsemane
Endear the shore beyond.
'Tis beggars banquets best define,
'Tis thirsting vitalizes wine.
Faith bleats to understand.

'He Fumbles at Your Soul'

He fumbles at your soul
As players at the keys
Before they drop full music on.
He stuns you by degrees,
Prepares your brittle nature
For the ethereal blow
By fainter hammers further heard,
Then nearer, then so slow
Your breath has time to straighten,
Your brain to bubble cool,
Deals one imperial thunderbolt
That scalps your naked soul.

When winds take forests in their paws
The universe is still.

'It Is an Honourable Thought'

It is an honourable thought
And makes one lift one's hat,
As one met sudden gentlefolk
Upon a daily street,
That we've immortal place
Though pyramids decay
And kingdoms like the orchard
Flit russetly away.

~

GERARD MANLEY HOPKINS
(1844–1889)

At Balliol College, Oxford, Hopkins became a disciple of Pusey and a member of the Anglo-Catholic wing of the Church of England. Dissatisfied with what he perceived as the anomalous nature of his position, he became a Roman Catholic in 1866, following in the footsteps of Newman who had taken the same step at Oxford twenty years earlier. He went on to become a Jesuit priest, a fact which shaped his poetic vision to a profound extent. As a result of the rigours of his Jesuit training he became thoroughly conversant with the philosophy of Duns Scotus and St Thomas Aquinas. The knowledge of scholastic philosophy shaped his notion of inscape, *the central concept at the heart of his work, and this in turn fused with a mystical love of nature to form the potent combination that makes his poetry so unique.*

Heaven-Haven
(A nun takes the veil)

I have desired to go
   Where springs not fail,
To fields where flies no sharp and sided hail
   And a few lilies blow.

And I have asked to be
   Where no storms come,
Where the green swell is in the havens dumb,
   And out of the swing of the sea.

Pied Beauty

Glory be to God for dappled things—
    For skies of couple-colour as a brinded cow;
        For rose-moles all in stipple upon trout that swim;
Fresh-firecoal chestnut-falls; finches' wings;
    Landscape plotted and pieced—fold, fallow, and plough;
        And all trades, their gear and tackle and trim.

All things counter, original, spare, strange;
    Whatever is fickle, freckled (who knows how?)
        With swift, slow; sweet, sour; adazzle, dim;
He fathers-forth whose beauty is past change:
    Praise him.

The Habit of Perfection

Elected Silence, sing to me
And beat upon my whorled ear,
Pipe me to pastures still and be
The music that I care to hear.

Shape nothing, lips; be lovely-dumb:
It is the shut, the curfew sent
From there where all surrenders come
Which only makes you eloquent.

Be shelled, eyes, with double dark
And find the uncreated light:
This ruck and reel which you remark
Coils, keeps, and teases simple sight.

Palate, the hutch of tasty lust,
Desire not to be rinsed with wine:
The can must be so sweet, the crust
So fresh that come in fasts divine!

Nostrils, your careless breath that spend
Upon the stir and keep of pride,
What relish shall the censers send
Along the sanctuary side!

O feel-of-primrose hands, O feet
That want the yield of plushy sward,
But you shall walk the golden street
And you unhouse and house the Lord.

And, Poverty, be thou the bride
And now the marriage feast begun,
And lily-coloured clothes provide
Your spouse not laboured-at nor spun.

God's Grandeur

The world is charged with the grandeur of God.
    It will flame out, like shining from shook foil;
    It gathers to a greatness, like the ooze of oil
Crushed. Why do men then now not reck his rod?
Generations have trod, have trod, have trod;
    And all is seared with trade; bleared, smeared with toil;
    And wears man's smudge and shares man's smell: the soil
Is bare now, nor can foot feel, being shod.

And, for all this, nature is never spent;
    There lives the dearest freshness deep down things;
And though the last lights off the black West went
    Oh, morning, at the brown brink eastward, springs—
Because the Holy Ghost over the bent
    World broods with warm breast and with ah! bright wings.

∼

As Kingfishers Catch Fire

As kingfishers catch fire, dragonflies draw flame;
 As tumbled over rim in roundy wells
 Stones ring; like each tucked string tells, each hung bell's
Bow swung finds tongue to fling out broad its name;
Each mortal thing does one thing and the same:
 Deals out that being indoors each one dwells;
 Selves—goes itself; *myself* it speaks and spells,
Crying *What I do is me: for that I came.*

I say more: the just man justices;
 Keeps grace: that keeps all his goings graces;
Acts in God's eye what in God's eye he is—
 Christ. For Christ plays in ten thousand places,
Lovely in limbs, and lovely in eyes not his
 To the Father through the features of men's faces.

Rosa Mystica

'The rose is a mystery'—where is it found,
Is it anything true? Does it grow upon ground?
It was made of earth's mould, but it went from men's eyes,
And its place is a secret and shut in the skies.
  In the gardens of God, in the daylight divine,
  Find me a place by thee, Mother of mine.

But where was it formerly? Which is the spot
That was blest in it once, though now it is not?
It is Galilee's growth: it grew at God's will
And broke into bloom upon Nazareth hill.
  In the gardens of God, in the daylight divine,
  I shall look on thy loveliness, Mother of mine.

What was its season, then? How long ago?
When was the summer that saw the bud blow?
Two thousands of years are near upon past
Since its birth and its bloom and its breathing its last.

In the gardens of God, in the daylight divine,
I shall keep time with thee, Mother of mine.

Tell me the name now, tell me its name.
The heart guesses easily: is it the same?
Mary the Virgin, well the heart knows,
She is the Mystery, she is the rose.
    In the gardens of God, in the daylight divine,
    I shall come home to thee, Mother of mine.

Is Mary the rose, then? Mary, the tree?
But the blossom, the blossom there—who can it be?
Who can her rose be? It could but be One:
Christ Jesus our Lord, her God and her Son.
    In the gardens of God, in the daylight divine,
    Show me thy Son, Mother, Mother of mine.

What was the colour of that blossom bright?—
White to begin with, immaculate white.
But what a wild flush on the flakes of it stood
When the rose ran in crimsonings down the cross-wood!
    In the gardens of God, in the daylight divine,
    I shall worship the wounds with thee, Mother of mine.

How many leaves had it?—Five they were then,
Five like the senses and members of men;
Five is their number by nature, but now
They multiply, multiply—who can tell how?
    In the gardens of God, in the daylight divine,
    Make me a leaf in thee, Mother of mine.

Does it smell sweet, too, in that holy place?
Sweet unto God, and the sweetness is grace:
The breath of it bathes great heaven above
In grace that is charity, grace that is love.
    To thy breast, to thy rest, to thy glory divine
    Draw me by charity, Mother of mine.

ALICE MEYNELL
(1847–1922)

*Alice and Wilfrid Meynell were two of the foremost figures in the lit-
erary life of late Victorian and Edwardian England. They edited sev-
eral periodicals and were largely responsible for popularising the poetry
of Coventry Patmore. They were also responsible for the rescue and
rehabilitation of Francis Thompson from a life of poverty and opium
addiction. Without their timely intervention it is likely that Thompson
would have died in wretched obscurity, without ever writing much of the
poetry for which he is now revered. As well as rendering these singular
services to poetry, Alice Meynell was a distinguished poet and essayist
in her own right.*

The Lady Poverty

The Lady Poverty was fair:
But she has lost her looks of late,
With change of times and change of air.
Ah slattern! she neglects her hair,
Her gown, her shoes; she keeps no state
As once when her pure feet were bare.

Or—almost worse, if worse can be—
She scolds in parlours, dusts and trims,
Watches and counts. O is this she
Whom Francis met, whose step was free,
Who with Obedience carolled hymns,
In Umbria walked with Chastity?

Where is her ladyhood? Not here,
Not among modern kinds of men;
But in the stony fields, where clear
Through the thin trees the skies appear,
In delicate spare soil and fen,
And slender landscape and austere.

In Portugal, 1912

And will they cast the altars down,
   Scatter the chalice, crush the bread?
In field, in village, and in town
   He hides an unregarded head;

Waits in the corn-lands far and near,
   Bright in His sun, dark in His frost,
Sweet in the vine, ripe in the ear—
   Lonely unconsecrated Host.

In ambush at the merry board
   The Victim lurks unsacrificed;
The mill conceals the harvest's Lord,
   The wine-press holds the unbidden Christ.

OSCAR WILDE
(1854–1900)

Wilde remains a controversial figure, as misunderstood today as he was in his own day. Such are the moral somersaults that society has performed in the century since his death that he is now vindicated for the very things for which he was vilified. Yet the central theme of Wilde's late works has little to do with the role of 'sexual liberator' which posterity has thrust upon him and everything to do with the repentant sinner seeking forgiveness. Wilde's 'heart of stone' was broken in Reading gaol and, although doubts persisted right until the very end, he was finally received into the Catholic Church on his deathbed. It is indeed ironic that Wilde is only remembered for the tragedy of his life and not for its happy ending.

E Tenebris

Come down, O Christ, and help me! reach thy hand,
    For I am drowning in a stormier sea
    Than Simon on thy lake of Galilee:
The wine of life is spilt upon the sand,
My heart is as some famine-murdered land
    Whence all good things have perished utterly
    And well I know my soul in Hell must lie
If I this night before God's throne should stand.
'He sleeps perchance, or rideth to the chase,
    Like Baal, when his prophets howled that name
    From morn to noon on Carmel's smitten height.'
Nay, peace, I shall behold, before the night,
    The feet of brass, the robe more white than flame,
The wounded hands, the weary human face.

From *The Ballad of Reading Gaol*

Like two doomed ships that pass in storm
    We had crossed each other's way:
But we made no sign, we said no word,
    We had no word to say;
For we did not meet in the holy night,
    But in the shameful day.

A prison wall was round us both,
    Two outcast men we were:
The world had thrust us from its heart,
    And God from out His care:
And the iron gin that waits for Sin
    Had caught us in its snare.

* * *

The grey cock crew, the red cock crew,
    But never came the day:
And crooked shapes of Terror crouched,
    In the corners where we lay:
And each evil sprite that walks by night
    Before us seemed to play.

They glided past, they glided fast,
    Like travellers through a mist:
They mocked the moon in a rigadoon
    Of delicate turn and twist,
And with formal pace and loathsome grace
    The phantoms kept their tryst.

With mop and mow, we saw them go,
    Slim shadows hand in hand:
About, about, in ghostly rout
    They trod a saraband:
And the damned grotesques made arabesques,
    Like the wind upon the sand!

With the pirouettes of marionettes,
    They tripped on pointed tread:
But with flutes of Fear they filled the ear,
    As their grisly masque they led,
And loud they sang, and long they sang,
    For they sang to wake the dead.

'Oho!' they cried, 'The world is wide,
    But fettered limbs go lame!
And once, or twice, to throw the dice
    Is a gentlemanly game,
But he does not win who plays with Sin
    In the secret House of Shame.'

No things of air these antics were,
    That frolicked with such glee:
To men whose lives were held in gyves,
    And whose feet might not go free,
Ah! wounds of Christ! they were living things
    Most terrible to see.

Around, around, they waltzed and wound;
    Some wheeled in smirking pairs;
With the mincing step of a demirep
    Some sidled up the stairs:
And with subtle sneer, and fawning leer,
    Each helped us at our prayers.

The morning wind began to moan,
    But still the night went on:
Through its giant loom the web of gloom
    Crept till each thread was spun:
And, as we prayed, we grew afraid
    Of the Justice of the Sun.

* * *

The warders strutted up and down,
  And watched their herd of brutes,
Their uniforms were spick and span,
  And they wore their Sunday suits,
But we knew the work they had been at,
  By the quicklime on their boots.

For where a grave had opened wide,
  There was no grave at all:
Only a stretch of mud and sand
  By the hideous prison-wall,
And a little heap of burning lime,
  That the man should have his pall.

* * *

For three long years they will not sow
  Or root or seedling there:
For three long years the unblessed spot
  Will sterile be and bare,
And look upon the wondering sky
  With unreproachful stare.

They think a murderer's heart would taint
  Each simple seed they sow.
It is not true! God's kindly earth
  Is kindlier than men know,
And the red rose would but blow more red,
  The white rose whiter blow.

Out of his mouth a red, red rose!
  Out of his heart a white!
For who can say by what strange way,
  Christ brings His will to light,
Since the barren staff the pilgrim bore
  Bloomed in the great Pope's sight?

But neither milk-white rose nor red
  May bloom in prison air;

The shard, the pebble, and the flint,
    Are what they give us there:
For flowers have been known to heal
    A common man's despair.

So never will wine-red rose or white,
    Petal by petal, fall
On that stretch of mud and sand that lies
    By the hideous prison-wall,
To tell the men who tramp the yard
    That God's son died for all.

Yet though the hideous prison-wall
    Still hems him round and round,
And a spirit may not walk by night
    That is with fetters bound,
And a spirit may but weep that lies
    In such unholy ground,

He is at peace—this wretched man—
    At peace, or will be soon:
There is not thing to make him mad,
    Nor does Terror walk at noon,
For the lampless Earth in which he lies
    Has neither Sun nor Moon.

They hanged him as a beast is hanged!
    They did not even toll
A requiem that might have brought
    Rest to his startled soul,
But hurriedly they took him out,
    And hid him in a hole.

The warders stripped him of his clothes,
    And gave him to the flies:
They mocked the swollen purple throat,
    And the stark and staring eyes:
And with laughter loud they heaped the shroud
    In which the convict lies.

The Chaplain would not kneel to pray
    By his dishonoured grave:
Nor mark it with that blessed Cross
    That Christ for sinners gave,
Because the man was one of those
    Whom Christ came down to save.

Yet all is well; he has but passed
    To Life's appointed bourne:
And alien tears will fill for him
    Pity's long-broken urn,
For his mourners will be outcast men,
    And outcasts always mourn.

* * *

And thus we rust Life's iron chain
    Degraded and alone:
And some men curse, and some men weep,
    And some men make no moan:
But God's eternal Laws are kind
    And break the heart of stone.

And every human heart that breaks,
    In prison-cell or yard,
Is as that broken box that gave
    Its treasure to the Lord,
And filled the unclean leper's house
    With the scent of costliest nard.

Ah! happy they whose hearts can break
    And peace of pardon win!
How else may man make straight his plan
    And cleanse his soul from Sin?
How else but through a broken heart
    May Lord Christ enter in?

* * *

And he of the swollen purple throat,
    And the stark and staring eyes,
Waits for the holy hands that took
    The Thief to Paradise;
And a broken and a contrite heart
    The Lord will not despise.

The man in red who reads the Law
    Gave him three weeks of life,
Three little weeks in which to heal
    His soul of his soul's strife,
And cleanse from every blot of blood
    The hand that held the knife.

And with tears of blood he cleansed the hand,
    The hand that held the steel:
For only blood can wipe out blood,
    And only tears can heal:
And the crimson stain that was of Cain
    Became Christ's snow-white seal.

~

FRANCIS THOMPSON
(1859–1907)

Like Oscar Wilde, Francis Thompson came to Christ via desolation. Born at Preston in Lancashire, his father was a doctor and his mother was the daughter of a surgeon. Both were Catholic converts. He trained for the priesthood at Ushaw College but was unsuited to the vocation and turned instead to medicine. Failing his medical examinations, he tried to join the army but was rejected as being medically unfit. In desperation, he fled to London in 1885 and for two years lived on the streets in post-Dickensian squalor. Much of the little money he earned, through selling matches or holding people's horses, he spent on his opium habit. He was rescued from this desperate situation by Wilfrid Meynell, husband of the poet Alice Meynell, who persuaded him to seek medical treatment. He spent two years at the Premonstratensian Monastery at Storrington in Sussex where much of his finest poetry was written. Three volumes of poetry were published between 1893 and 1897 to immediate critical acclaim.

~

'In No Strange Land'

O world invisible, we view thee,
O world intangible, we touch thee,
O world unknowable, we know thee,
Inapprehensible, we clutch thee!

Does the fish soar to find the ocean,
The eagle plunge to find the air—
That we ask of the stars in motion
If they have rumour of thee there?

Not where the wheeling systems darken,
And our benumbed conceiving soars!—
The drift of pinions, would we hearken,
Beats at our own clay-shuttered doors.

The angels keep their ancient places;—
Turn but a stone, and start a wing!
'Tis ye, 'tis your estranged faces,
That miss the many-splendoured thing.

But (when so sad thou canst not sadder)
Cry;—and upon thy so sore loss
Shall shine the traffic of Jacob's ladder
Pitched betwixt Heaven and Charing Cross.

Yea, in the night, my Soul, my daughter,
Cry,—clinging Heaven by the hems;
And lo, Christ walking on the water
Not of Gennesareth, but Thames!

The Hound of Heaven

I fled Him, down the nights and down the days:
I fled Him, down the arches of the years;
I fled Him, down the labyrinthine way
　　Of my own mind; and in the mist of tears
I hid from Him, and under running laughter.
　　　　Up vistaed hopes I sped;
　　　　And shot, precipitated,
Adown Titanic glooms of chasmed fears,
　　From those strong Feet that followed, followed after.
　　　　But with unhurrying chase,
　　　　And unperturbed pace,
　　Deliberate speed, majestic instancy,
　　　　They beat—and a Voice beat
　　　　More instant than the Feet—
'All things betray thee, who betrayest Me.'

　　　　I pleaded, outlaw-wise,
By many a hearted casement, curtained red,
　　Trellised with intertwining charities;
(For, though I knew His love Who followed,
　　　　Yet was I sore adread
Lest, having Him, I must have naught beside)
But, if one little casement parted wide,
　　The gust of His approach would clash it to:
　　Fear wist not to evade, as Love wist to pursue.

Across the margent of the world I fled,
　　And troubled the gold gateways of the stars,
　　Smiting for shelter on their clanged bars;
　　　　Fretted to dulcet jars
And silvern chatter the pale ports o' the moon.
I said to Dawn: Be sudden—to Eve: Be soon;
　　With thy young skiey blossoms heap me over
　　　　From this tremendous Lover—
Float thy vague veil about me, lest He see!

I tempted all His servitors, but to find
My own betrayal in their constancy,
In faith to Him their fickleness to me,
    Their traitorous trueness, and their loyal deceit.
To all swift things for swiftness did I sue;
    Clung to the whistling mane of every wind.
But whether they swept, smoothly fleet,
    The long savannahs of the blue;
        Or whether, Thunder-driven,
    They clanged his chariot 'thwart a heaven,
Plashy with flying lightnings round the spurn o' their feet:—
    Fear wist not to evade as Love wist to pursue.
        Still with unhurrying chase,
        And unperturbed pace,
    Deliberate speed, majestic instancy,
        Came on the following Feet,
        And a Voice above their beat—
'Naught shelters thee, who wilt not shelter Me.'

I sought no more that after which I strayed
        In face of man or maid;
But still within the little children's eyes
        Seems something, something that replies,
They at least are for me, surely for me!
I turned me to them very wistfully;
But just as their young eyes grew sudden fair
        With dawning answers there,
Their angel plucked them from me by the hair.
'Come then, ye other children, Nature's—share
With me' (said I) 'your delicate fellowship;
        Let me greet you lip to lip,
        Let me twine with you caresses,
            Wantoning
        With our Lady-Mother's vagrant tresses,
            Banqueting
        With her in her wind-walled palace,

Underneath her azured dais,
    Quaffing, as your taintless way is,
        From a chalice
Lucent-weeping out of the dayspring.'
        So it was done:
I in their delicate fellowship was one—
Drew the bolt of Nature's secrecies.
        I knew all the swift importings
        On the wilful face of skies;
        I knew how the clouds arise
        Spumed of the wild sea-snortings;
            All that's born or dies
Rose and drooped with; made them shapers
Of mine own moods, or wailful or divine;
        With them joyed and was bereaven.
        I was heavy with the even,
        When she lit her glimmering tapers
        Round the day's dead sanctities.
        I laughed in the morning's eyes.
I triumphed and I saddened with all weather,
        Heaven and I wept together,
And its sweet tears were salt with mortal mine;
Against the red throb of its sunset-heart
        I laid my own to beat,
        And share commingling heat;
But not by that, by that, was eased my human smart.
In vain my tears were wet on Heaven's grey cheek.
For ah! we know not what each other says,
        These things and I; in sound *I* speak—
Their sound is but their stir, they speak by silences.
Nature, poor stepdame, cannot slake my drouth;
        Let her, if she would owe me,
Drop yon blue blossom-veil of sky, and show me
        The breasts of her tenderness:
Never did any milk of hers once bless
        My thirsting mouth.

Nigh and nigh draws the chase,
    With unperturbed pace,
Deliberate speed, majestic instancy;
    And past those noised Feet
    A Voice comes yet more fleet—
'Lo! naught contents thee, who content'st not Me.'

Naked I wait Thy love's uplifted stroke!
My harness piece by piece Thou hast hewn from me,
    And smitten me to my knee;
    I am defenceless utterly.
    I slept, methinks, and woke,
And, slowly gazing, find me stripped in sleep.
In the rash lustihead of my young powers,
    I shook the pillaring hours
And pulled my life upon me; grimed with smears,
I stand amid the dust o' the mounded years—
My mangled youth lies dead beneath the heap.
My days have crackled and gone up in smoke,
Have puffed and burst as sun-starts on a stream.
    Yea, faileth now even dream
The dreamer, and the lute the lutanist;
Even the linked fantasies, in whose blossomy twist
I swung the earth a trinket at my wrist,
Are yielding; cords of all too weak account
For earth with heavy griefs so overplussed.
    Ah! is Thy love indeed
A weed, albeit an amaranthine weed,
Suffering no flowers except its own to mount?
        Ah! must—
        Designer infinite!—
Ah! must Thou char the wood ere Thou canst limn with it?
My freshness spent its wavering shower i' the dust;
And now my heart is as a broken fount,
Wherein tear-drippings stagnate, spilt down ever
    From the dank thoughts that shiver

Upon the sighful branches of my mind.
        Such is; what is to be?
The pulp so bitter, how shall taste the rind?
I dimly guess what Time in mists confounds;
Yet ever and anon a trumpet sounds
From the hid battlements of Eternity;
Those shaken mists a space unsettle, then
Round the half-glimpsed turrets slowly wash again.
        But not ere him who summoneth
        I first have seen enwound
With glooming robes purpureal, cypress-crowned;
His name I know, and what his trumpet saith.
Whether man's heart or life it be which yields
        Thee harvest, must Thy harvest-fields
        Be dunged with rotten death?
            Now of that long pursuit
            Comes on at hand the bruit;
        That Voice is round me like a bursting sea:
            'And is thy earth so marred,
            Shattered in shard on shard?
            Lo, all things fly thee, for thou fliest Me!
        'Strange, piteous, futile thing!
Wherefore should any set thee love apart?
Seeing none but I makes much of naught' (He said),
'And human love needs human meriting:
        How hast thou merited—
Of all man's clotted clay the dingiest clot?
        Alack, thou knowest not
How little worthy of any love thou art!
Whom wilt thou find to love ignoble thee,
        Save Me, save only Me?
All which I took from thee I did but take,
        Not for thy harms,
But just that thou which might'st seek it in My arms.
        All which thy child's mistake
Fancies as lost, I have stored for thee at home:
        Rise, clasp My hand, and come!'

Halts by me that footfall:
　　Is my gloom, after all,
Shade of His hand, outstretched caressingly?
　　'Ah, fondest, blindest, weakest,
　　I am He Whom thou seekest!
Thou dravest love from thee, who dravest Me.'

～

Love and the Child

'Why do you so clasp me,
　　And draw me to your knee?
Forsooth, you do but chafe me,
　　I pray you let me be:
I will be loved but now and then
　　When it liketh me!'

So I heard a young child,
　　A thwart child, a young child
Rebellious against love's arms,
　　Make its peevish cry.

To the tender God I turn:—
　　'Pardon, Love most High!
For I think those arms were even Thine,
　　And that child even I.'

Lines for a Drawing of Our Lady of the Night

This, could I paint my inward sight,
This were Our Lady of the Night:

She bears on her front's lucency
The starlight of her purity:

For as the white rays of that star
The union of all colours are,

She sums all virtues that may be
In her sweet light of purity.

The mantle which she holds on high
Is the great mantle of the sky.

Think, O sick toiler, when the night
Comes on thee, sad and infinite,

Think, sometimes, 'tis our own Lady
Spreads her blue mantle over thee,

And folds the earth, a wearied thing,
Beneath its gentle shadowing;

Then rest a little; and in sleep
Forget to weep, forget to weep!

A Dead Astronomer
Stephen Perry, SJ

Starry amorist, starward gone,
Thou art—what thou didst gaze upon!
Passed through thy golden garden's bars,
Thou seest the Gardener of the Stars.
She, about whose mooned brows
Seven stars make seven glows,
Seven lights for seven woes;
She, like thine own Galaxy,
All lustres in one purity:—
What said'st thou, Astronomer,
When thou did'st discover *her*?
When thy hand its tube let fall,
Thou found'st the fairest Star of all!

New Year's Chimes

What is the song the stars sing?
  (*And a million songs are as song of one*)
This is the song the stars sing:
  (*Sweeter song's none*)

One to set, and many to sing,
  (*And a million songs are as song of one*)
One to stand, and many to cling,
The many things, and the one Thing,
  The one that runs not, the many that run.

The ever new weaveth the ever old,
  (*And a million songs are as song of one*)
Ever telling the never told;
The silver saith, and the said is gold,
  And done ever the never done,

The Chase that's chased is the Lord o' the chase,
  (*And a million songs are as song of one*)
And the Pursued cries on the race;
And the hounds in leash are the hounds that run.

Hidden stars by the shown stars' sheen;
  (*And a million suns are but as one*)
Colours unseen by the colours seen,
And sounds unheard heard sounds between,
  And a night is in the light of the sun.

An ambuscade of light in night,
  (*And a million secrets are but as one*)
And a night is dark in the sun's light,
  And a world in the world man looks upon.

Hidden stars by the shown stars' wings,
  (*And a million cycles are but as one*)
And a world with unapparent strings
Knits the simulant world of things;
  Behold and vision thereof is none.

The world above in the world below,
  (*And a million worlds are but as one*)
And the One in all; as the sun's strength so
Strives in all strength, glows in all glow
    Of the earth that wits not, and man thereon.

Braced in its own fourfold embrace
  (*And a million strengths are as strength of one*)
And round it all God's arms of grace,
The world, so as the Vision says,
    Doth with great lightning-tramples run.

And thunder bruiteth into thunder,
  (*And a million sounds are as sound of one*)
From stellate peak to peak is tossed a voice of wonder,
And the height stoops down to the depths thereunder,
    And sun leans forth to his brother-sun.

And the more ample years unfold
  (*With a million songs as song of one*)
A little new of the ever old,
A little told of the never told,
    Added act of the never done.

Loud the descant, and low the theme,
  (*A million songs are as song of one*)
And the dream of the world is dream in dream,
But the one Is is, or nought could seem;
    And the song runs round to the song begun.

This is the song the stars sing,
  (*Toned all in time*)
Tintinnabulous, tuned to ring
A multitudinous-single thing
  (*Rung all in rhyme*).

To a Snowflake

What heart could have thought you?—
Past our devisal
(O filigree petal!)
Fashioned so purely,
Fragilely, surely,
From what Paradisal
Imagineless metal,
Too costly for cost?
Who hammered you, wrought you,
From argentine vapour?—
'God was my shaper.
Passing surmisal,
He hammered, He wrought me,
From curled silver vapour,
To lust of His mind:—
Thou could'st not have thought me!
So purely, so palely,
Tinily, surely,
Mightily, frailly,
Insculped and embossed,
With His hammer of wind,
And His graver of frost.'

St Monica

At the Cross thy station keeping
With the mournful Mother weeping,
Thou, unto the sinless Son,
Weepest for thy sinful one.
Blood and water from His side
Gush; in thee the streams divide:
From thine eyes the one doth start,
But the other from thy heart.

Mary, for thy sinner, see,
To her Sinless mourns with thee:
Could that Son the son not heed,
For whom two such mothers plead?
So thy child had baptism twice,
And the whitest from thine eyes.

The floods lift up, lift up their voice,
With a many-watered noise!
Down the centuries fall those sweet
Sobbing waters to our feet,
And our laden air still keeps
Murmur of a Saint that weeps.

Teach us but, to grace our prayers,
Such divinity of tears,—
Earth should be lustrate again
With contrition of that rain:
Till celestial floods o'er-rise
The high tops of Paradise.

~

Motto and Invocation

Omnia per ipsum, et sine ipso nihil.

Pardon, O Saint John divine,
That I change a word of thine.
None the less, aid thou me!
And Siena's Catherine;
Lofty doctor, Augustine,
Glorious penitent; and be
Assisi's Francis also mine!
Mine be Padua's Anthony,
And that other Francis, he
Called of Sales—Let all combine
And counsel of great charity
What I write! Thy wings incline,
O my Angel, o'er the line!
Last and first, O Queen Mary,
And thy white Immaculacy,
If my work may profit aught
Fill with lilies every thought!
   I surmise
What is white will then be wise.
   To which I add
Thomas More
Teach (thereof my need is sore)
What thou showedst well on earth—
Good writ, good wit, make goodly mirth!

NORMAN GALE
(1862–1926)

The Country Faith

Here in the country's heart
Where the grass is green,
Life is the same sweet life
As it e'er hath been.

Trust in a God still lives,
And the bell at morn
Floats with a thought of God
O'er the rising corn.

God comes down in the rain,
And the crop grows tall—
This is the country faith,
And the best of all.

HILAIRE BELLOC
(1870–1953)

Hilaire Belloc and G. K. Chesterton were at the forefront of what the publisher F. J. Sheed called the 'Catholic Intellectual Revival'. Bernard Shaw, a friend of both men, dubbed them the 'Chesterbelloc' as a jocular reference to what was perceived as their inseparability. H. G. Wells complained that the two men had placed a 'boozy halo' around Catholicism, a reference to their rumbustious joie de vivre *and their idolising and idealising of a pre-industrial Merrie England. Belloc was a highly versatile man of letters, writing essays, novels, biographies, historical studies and many poems of considerable merit.*

The End of the Road

In these boots and with this staff
Two hundred leaguers and a half
Walked I, went I, paced I, tripped I,
Marched I, held I, skelped I, slipped I,
Pushed I, panted, swung and dashed I;
Picked I, forded, swam and splashed I,
Strolled I, climbed I, crawled and scrambled,
Dropped and dipped I, ranged and rambled;
Plodded I, hobbled I, trudged and tramped I,
And in lonely spinnies camped I,
And in haunted pinewoods slept I,
Lingered, loitered, limped and crept I,
Clambered, halted, stepped and leapt I;
Slowly sauntered, roundly strode I,
And . . .   (Oh, Patron saints and Angels
                That protect the four Evangels!
                And you Prophets vel majores

Vel incerti, vel minores,
Virgines ac confessores
Chief of whose peculiar glories
Est in Aula Regis stare
Atque orare et exorare
Et clamare et conclamare
Clamantes cum clamoribus
Pro Nobis Peccatoribus.)
Let me not conceal it . . . *Rode I.*
(For who but critics could complain
Of 'riding' in a railway train?)
Across the valleys and the high-land,
With all the world on either hand,
Drinking when I had a mind to,
Singing when I felt inclined to;
Nor ever turned my face to home
Till I had slaked my heart at Rome.

Twelfth Night

As I was lifting over Down
A winter's night to Petworth Town,
I came upon a company
Of Travellers who would talk with me.

The riding moon was small and bright,
They cast no shadows in her light:
There was no man for miles a-near.
I would not walk with them for fear.

A star in heaven by Gumber glowed,
An ox across the darkness lowed,
Whereat a burning light there stood
Right in the heart of Gumber Wood.

Across the rime their marching rang,
And in a little while they sang;
They sang a song I used to know,
  Gloria
In Excelsis Domino.

The frozen way those people trod
It led towards the Mother of God;
Perhaps if I had travelled with them
I might have come to Bethlehem.

Rose

Rose, little Rose, the youngest of the Roses,
My little Rose whom I may never see,
When you shall come to where the heart reposes
Cut me a Rose and send it down to me.

When you shall come into the High Rose-Gardens,
Where Roses bend upon Our Lady's Tree,
The place of Plenitudes, the place of Pardons,
Cut me a Rose and send it down to me.

∼

ROBERT HUGH BENSON
(1871–1914)

As the son of an Archbishop of Canterbury, Benson's reception into the Catholic Church in 1903 caused a national sensation. Rarely since Newman's controversial conversion half a century earlier had anything aroused such scandal in ecclesiastical circles. There were other notable parallels between Benson and Newman. Both were Anglican clergymen at the time of their reception into the Church and both were ordained as Catholic priests after short periods of study in Rome. Like Newman, Benson wrote an apologia explaining the reasons behind his conversion. His Confessions of a Convert *was published in 1913, shortly before his untimely death the following year. In his short life he wrote a number of best-selling novels and his* Spiritual Letters, *published posthumously, exhibit the depth of his faith. He also wrote several poems, also published posthumously.*

Lines Written before August 1903

I cannot soar and sing my Lord and love;
　　No eagle's wings have I,
No power to rise and greet my King above,
　　No heart to fly.
Creative Lord Incarnate, let me lean
　　My heavy self on Thee;
Nor let my utter weakness come between
　　Thy strength and me.

I cannot trace Thy Providence and place,
　　Nor dimly comprehend
What in Thyself Thou art, and what is man,
　　And what the end.
Here in this wilderness I cannot find
　　The path the Wise Men trod;

Grant me to rest on Thee, Incarnate Mind
    And Word of God.

I cannot love, my heart is turned within
    And locked within; (Ah me!
How shivering in self-love I sit) for sin
    Has lost the key.
Ah! Sacred Heart of Jesus, Flame divine,
    Ardent with great desire,
My hope is set upon that love of Thine,
    Deep Well of Fire.

I cannot live alone another hour;
    Jesu, be Thou my Life!
I have not power to strive; be Thou my Power
    In every strife!
I can do nothing—hope, nor love, nor fear,
    But only fail and fall.
Be Thou my soul and self, O Jesu dear,
    My God and all!

A Halt

Lie still, my soul, the Sun of Grace
Is warm within this garden space
    Beneath tall kindly trees.
The quiet light is green and fair;
A fragrance fills the swooning air;
    Lie still, and take thine ease.

This silent noon of Jesu's love
Is warm about thee and above—
    A tender Lord is He.
Lie still an hour—this place is His.
He has a thousand pleasaunces,
And each all fair and fragrant is,
    And each is all for thee.

Then, Jesu, for a little space
I rest me in this garden place,
   All sweet to scent and sight.
Here, from this high-road scarce withdrawn,
I thrust my hot hands in the lawn
Cool yet with dew of far-off dawn
   And saturate with light.

But ah, dear Saviour, human-wise,
I yearn to pierce all mysteries,
To catch Thine Hands, and see Thine Eyes
   When evening sounds begin.
There, in Thy white Robe, Thou wilt wait
At dusk beside some orchard gate,
And smile to see me come so late,
   And, smiling, call me in.

The Invitation

Lord take Thine ease within my heart,
   Rest here and count Thyself at home;
Do as Thou wilt; rise, set, depart;
My master, not my guest, Thou art;
   Come as Thou wilt, but come, Lord, come.

Do Thine own pleasure. Surely, Lord,
   Thou art full free to come and go,
To lift my sorrow by a word,
Or pierce me with a sudden sword,
   And leave me sobbing in my woe.

Come in broad day, for good or ill,
   In time of business or of prayer;
Come in disguise, if so Thy will
Be better served, that I may still
   Wait on my Lord, though unaware.

Come with the dawn, shine in on me
   And wake my soul with welcome light;

Or let the twilight herald Thee,
And falling dusk Thy shelter be
    To shroud Thy coming from my sight.

Come by the way beneath the trees
    Where whispering heath and bracken stir;
There, where my spirit takes her ease,
Let that pure scented evening breeze
    Waft me the aloes and the myrrh.

Come, tender Lover, still and bright,
    Rose crowned and framed in gracious form;
Or come with terror, and by night,
Thundrous and girt with vivid light,
    A giant striding with the storm.

Come through the Cloister, past the lawn
    And laurels where the thin jet plays;
Where, from the wrangling world withdrawn,
Waking to silence dawn by dawn,
    My soul comes forth to studious days.

Come through the carven door, and bring
    A burst of Music through to me;
One chord of organ-thundering
And measured song of those that sing,
    Dear Saviour, to the praise of Thee.

Or come by some forgotten way
    Untrodden long and overgrown;
And on a sudden on a day
Burst in; snap web and ivy spray
    That claim the entrance for their own.

So many doors, and all divine,
    And every latch is loose to Thee.
So many paths, and all are Thine
That bring Thee to this heart of mine,
    And all are therefore dear to me!

O Deus Ego Amo Te

O God, I love Thee mightily,
Not only for Thy saving me,
Nor yet because who love not Thee
Must burn throughout eternity.
Thou, Thou, my Jesu, once didst me
Embrace upon the bitter Tree.
For me the nails, the soldier's spear,
With injury and insult, bear—
In pain all pain exceeding,
In sweating and in bleeding,
Yea, very death, and that for me
   A sinner all unheeding!
O Jesu, should I not love Thee
Who thus hast dealt so lovingly—
Not hoping some reward to see,
Nor lest I my damnation be;
But, as Thyself hast loved me,
So love I now and always Thee,
Because my King alone Thou art,
Because, O God, mine own Thou art!

Wedding Hymn

Father, within Thy House today
   We wait Thy kindly love to see;
Since thou hast said in truth that they
   Who dwell in love are one with Thee,
Bless those who for Thy blessing wait,
Their love accept and consecrate.

Dear Lord of love, whose Heart of Fire,
   So full of pity for our sin,
Was once in that Divine Desire
   Broken, Thy Bride to woo and win:

Look down and bless them from above
And keep their hearts alight with love.

Blest Spirit, who with life and light
    Didst quicken chaos to Thy praise,
Whose energy, in sin's despite,
    Still lifts our nature up to grace;
Bless those who here in troth consent.
Creator, crown Thy Sacrament.

Great One in Three, of Whom are named
    All families in earth and heaven,
Hear us, who have Thy promise claimed,
    And let a wealth of grace be given;
Grant them in life and death to be
Each knit to each, and both to Thee.

After a Retreat

What hast thou learnt today?
Hast thou sounded awful mysteries,
Hast pierced the veiled skies,
Climbed to the feet of God,
Trodden where saints have trod,
Fathomed the heights above?
    Nay,
This only have I learnt, that God is love.

What hast thou heard today?
Hast heard the Angel-trumpets cry,
And rippling harps reply;
Heard from the Throne of flame
Whence God incarnate came
Some thund'rous message roll?
    Nay,
This have I heard, His voice within my soul.

What hast thou felt today?
The pinions of the Angel guide
That standeth at thy side
In rapturous ardours beat,
Glowing, from head to feet,
In ecstasy divine?
    Nay,
This only have felt, Christ's hand in mine.

~

G. K. CHESTERTON
(1874-1936)

To the young people of my generation G.K.C. was a kind of Christian liberator. Like a beneficent bomb, he blew out of the Church a quantity of stained glass of a very poor period, and let in gusts of fresh air in which the dead leaves of doctrine danced with all the energy and indecorum of Our Lady's Tumbler.

Dorothy L. Sayers

Chesterton was probably the most influential Christian writer in England during the first third of the twentieth century. In books such as Orthodoxy *and* The Everlasting Man, *and biographies of St Francis of Assisi and St Thomas Aquinas, he expressed the tenets of the faith in a lively and lucid fashion. Like Belloc, he was a highly versatile man of letters whose literary output included essays, novels, detective stories, biographies and, last but not least, poetry.*

A Hymn

O God of earth and altar,
   Bow down and hear our cry,
Our earthly rulers falter,
   Our people drift and die;
The walls of gold entomb us,
   The swords of scorn divide,
Take not thy thunder from us
   But take away our pride.

From all that terror teaches,
   From lies of tongue and pen,

From all the easy speeches
   That comfort cruel men,
For sale and profanation
   Of honour and the sword,
From sleep and from damnation,
   Deliver us, good Lord.

Tie in a living tether
   The prince and priest and thrall,
Bind all our lives together,
   Smite us and save us all;
In ire and exultation
   Aflame with faith, and free,
Lift up a living nation,
   A single sword to thee.

The Skeleton

Chattering finch and water-fly
Are not merrier than I;
Here among the flowers I lie
Laughing everlastingly.
No: I may not tell the best;
Surely, friends, I might have guessed
Death was but the good King's jest,
   It was hid so carefully.

~

MAURICE BARING

(1874–1945)

Baring's friendship with Belloc and Chesterton has been immortalised in Sir James Gunn's portrait of the three men which can still be seen in the National Portrait Gallery. Through his relationship with Belloc, and later with Chesterton, Baring overcame his scepticism and embraced Christianity. His sonnet sequence, Vita Nuova, *celebrates his reception into the Catholic Church on the eve of Candlemas 1909, which Baring later described as 'the only action in my life which I am quite certain I have never regretted'. Perhaps his most moving testament in verse is his short poem 'My Body Is a Broken Toy'. The first verse was written in 1937 when he had become seriously ill with Parkinson's disease; the second verse, written four years later when his condition had deteriorated considerably, is a hymn of hope.*

Candlemas

The town is half awake; the nave, the choir,
Are dark, and all is dim, within, without;
But every chapel fringed with the devout,
Is bright with February flowers of fire.

At Mass, a thousand years ago in Rome,
Thus Priest, thus Server at the altar bowed;
Thus knelt, thus blessed itself the kneeling crowd,
At Dawn, within the secret catacomb.

Thus shall they meet for Mass, until the day
The glory of the world shall pass away.
And beauty far away from human reach,

And power, and wealth beyond all mortal price,
And glory that outsoars all thought, all speech,
Speak in the whispered words of sacrifice.

Vita Nuova

I

I found the clue I sought not in the night,
While wandering in a pathless maze of gloom;
The sky was hid behind huge shapes of doom;
There was no moon, nor any star in sight.

My hopes, my dreams, and my faithless creeds were slain,
Like corpses on a battlefield they lay;
The world was but a graveyard dark with clay;
The stifling cloud denied one drop of rain;

When from the giddy marge of the abyss,
I cried aloud in agony and fear,
When, suddenly, it seemed my single tear
Stretched and became a shining bridge to bliss.

I stood before a topless gate. Within
I guessed the light, I dared not enter in.

II

One day I heard a whisper: 'Wherefore wait?
Why linger in a separated porch?
Why nurse the flicker of a severed torch?
The fire is there, ablaze beyond the gate.

Why tremble, foolish soul? Why hesitate?
However faint the knock, it will be heard.'
I knocked, and swiftly came the answering word,
Which bade me enter to my own estate.

I found myself in a familiar place;
And there my broken soul began to mend;
I knew the smile of every long-lost face—

They whom I had forgot remembered me;
I knelt, I knew—it was too bright to see—
The welcome of a King who was my friend.

My treasure and my resting-place are found,
My mother-land, my immemorial home;
Beyond the reefs of treasonable foam,
I know the lights that flash upon the sound.

Lightning may strike, and hurricane may blow,
Whatever shall befall, I cannot fear:
Whether the hour be far away or near,
The tranquil harbour shines and waits, I know.

I know. There is no mortal word to say;
For what there is to speak is vast and dim;
But haply, if God please, beyond the day,

Delivered from the bars and bonds of speech,
Made strong with language which the angels teach,
I'll share my secret with the Seraphim.

My Body Is a Broken Toy

My body is a broken toy
Which nobody can mend
Unfit for either play or ploy
My body is a broken toy;
But all things end.
The siege of Troy
Came one day to an end.
My body is a broken toy
Which nobody can mend.

My soul is an immortal toy
Which nobody can mar,
An instrument of praise and joy;
My soul is an immortal toy;
Though rusted from the world's alloy
It glitters like a star;
My soul is an immortal toy
Which nobody can mar.

ALFRED NOYES
(1880–1958)

Although one of the most popular poets of the Edwardian period, Alfred Noyes was considered Victorian, and therefore old-fashioned, by the new generation of poets, spearheaded by T. S. Eliot and Edith Sitwell, who rose to prominence in the early 1920s. Noyes's verse had more in common with Tennyson than with poetry's new wave and he represented the reactionary rearguard against the 'modernists'. At its height, the battle of words between Noyes and Sitwell was both intense and ill tempered. The triumph of the modernists led to Noyes's fall from favour and his becoming synonymous with all that was unfashionable in English verse. As a result his reputation suffered and his achievement was eclipsed. Today he is largely forgotten. Ironically, Noyes, Sitwell and Eliot all responded to the ills of the twentieth century in much the same way, seeking solutions in traditional Christianity. Noyes and Sitwell both became converts to Catholicism while Eliot became a celebrated champion of Anglo-Catholicism within the Church of England.

The Old Sceptic

I am weary of disbelieving: why should I wound my love
    To pleasure a sophist's pride in a graven image of truth?
I will go back to my home, with the clouds and the stars above,
    And the heaven I used to know, and the God of my buried
      youth.

I will go back to the home where of old in my boyish pride
    I pierced my father's heart with a murmur of unbelief.
He only looked in my face as I spoke, but his mute eyes cried
    Night after night in my dreams; and he died in grief, in grief.

Books? I have read the books, the books that we write ourselves,
    Extolling our love of an abstract truth and our pride of debate:
I will go back to the love of the cotter who sings as he delves,
    To that childish infinite love and the God above fact and date.

To that ignorant infinite God who colours the meaningless
    flowers,
    To that lawless infinite Poet who crowns the law with the
        crime;
To the Weaver who covers the world with a garment of
    wonderful hours,
    And holds in His hand like threads the tales and the truths of
        time.

Is the faith of the cotter so simple and narrow as this? Ah, well,
    It is hardly so narrow as yours who daub and plaster with
        dyes
The shining mirrors of heaven, the shadowy mirrors of hell,
    And blot out the dark deep vision, if it seemed to be framed
        with lies.

No faith I hurl against you, no fact to freeze your sneers.
    Only the doubt you taught me to weld in the fires of youth
Leaps to my hand like the flaming sword of nineteen hundred
    years,
    The sword of the high God's answer, *O Pilate, what is truth?*

Your laughter has killed more hearts than ever were pierced
    with swords,
    Ever you daub new mirrors and turn the old ot the wall;
And more than blood is lost in the weary battle of words;
    For creeds are many; but God is One, and contains them all.

Ah, why should we strive or cry? Surely the end is close!
    Hold by your little truths: deem your triumph complete!
But nothing is true or false in the infinite heart of the rose;
    And the earth is a little dust that clings to our travelling feet.

I will go back to my home and look at the wayside flowers,
    And hear from the wayside cabins the kind old hymns again,
Where Christ holds out His arms in the quiet evening hours,
    And the light of the chapel porches broods on the peaceful
    lane.

And there I shall hear men praying the deep old foolish prayers,
   And there I shall see, once more, the fond old faith confessed,
And the strange old light on their faces who hear as a blind man
      hears,—
   Come unto Me, ye weary, and I will give you rest.

I will go back and believe in the deep old foolish tales,
   And pray the simple prayers that I learned at my mother's
      knee
Where the Sabbath tolls its peace thro' the breathless
      mountain-vales,
   And the sunset's evening hymn hallows the listening sea.

From *Vicisti, Galilaee*

Not ours to scorn the first white gleam
   Of beauty on this earth,
The clouds of dawn, the nectarous dream,
   The gods of simpler birth;
But, as ye praise them, your own cry
   Is fraught with deeper pain,
And the Compassionate ye deny
   Returns, returns again.

O worshippers of the beautiful,
   Is this the end then, this,—
That ye can only see the skull
   Beneath the face of bliss?
No monk in the dark years ye scorn
   So barren a pathway trod
As ye who, ceasing not to mourn,
   Deny the mourner's God.

And, while ye scoff, on every side
   Great hints of Him go by,—
Souls that are hourly crucified
   On some new Calvary!

O, tortured face, white and meek,
  Half seen amidst the crowd,
Grey suffering lips that never speak,
  The Glory in the Cloud!

In flower and dust, in chaff and grain,
  He binds Himself and dies!
We live by His eternal pain,
  His hourly sacrifice:
The limits of our mortal life
  Are His. The whisper thrills
Under the sea's perpetual strife,
  And through the sunburnt hills.

Darkly, as in a glass, our sight
  Still gropes thro' Time and Space:
We cannot see the Light of Light
  With angels, face to face:
Only the tale His martyrs tell
  Around the dark earth rings
He died and He went down to hell
  And lives—the King of Kings!

Ay, while ye scoff, from shore to shore,
  From sea to moaning sea,
Eloi, Eloi, goes up once more
  Lama sabacthani!
The heavens are like a scroll unfurled,
  The writing flames above—
This is the King of all the world
  Upon His Cross of Love.

On the Death of Francis Thompson

How grandly glow the bays
  Purpureally enwound
With those rich thorns, the brows
  How infinitely crowned
That now thro' Death's dark house
  Have passed with royal gaze:
Purpureally enwound
  How grandly glow the bays.

Sweet, sweet and three-fold sweet,
  Pulsing with three-fold pain,
Where the lark fails of flight
  Soared the celestial strain;
Beyond the sapphire height
  Flew the gold-winged feet,
Beautiful, pierced with pain,
  Sweet, sweet and three-fold sweet;

And where *Is not* and *Is*
  Are wed in one sweet Name,
And the world's rootless vine
  With dew of stars a-flame
Laughs, from those deep divine
  Impossibilities,
Our reason all to shame—
  This cannot be, but is;

Into the Vast, the Deep
  Beyond all mortal sight,
The Nothingness that conceived
  The worlds of day and night,
The Nothingness that heaved
  Pure sides in virgin sleep,
Brought out of Darkness, light;
  And man from out the Deep.

Into that Mystery
    Let not thine hand be thrust:
Nothingness is a world
    Thy science well may trust . . .
But lo, a leaf unfurled,
    Nay, a cry mocking thee
From the first grain of dust—
    I am, yet cannot be!

Adventuring unafraid
    Into that last deep shrine;
Must not the child-heart see
    Its deepest symbol shine,
The world's Birth-mystery,
    Whereto the suns are shade?
Lo, the white breast divine—
    The Holy Mother-maid!

How miss that Sacrifice,
    That cross of Yea and Nay,
That paradox of heaven
    Whose palms point either way,
Through each a nail being driven
    That the arms out-span the skies
And our earth-dust this day
    Out-sweeten Paradise.

We part the seamless robe,
    Our wisdom would divide
The raiment of the King,
    Our spear is in His side,
Even while the angels sing
    Around our perishing globe,
And Death re-knits in pride
    The seamless purple robe.

How grandly glow the bays
   Purpureally enwound
With those rich thorns, the brows
   How infinitely crowned
That now thro' Death's dark house
   Have passed with royal gaze:
Purpureally enwound
   How grandly glow the bays.

To a Pessimist

Life like a cruel mistress woos
   The passionate heart of man, you say,
Only in mockery to refuse
   His love, at last, and turn away.

To me she seems a queen that knows
   How great is love—but ah, how rare!—
And, pointing heavenward ere she goes,
   Gives him the rose from out her hair.

~

SIEGFRIED SASSOON
(1886–1967)

Siegfried Sassoon was a septuagenarian when he was received into the Catholic Church in 1957. An early and lasting admiration for Belloc and a late friendship with Ronald Knox were both significant factors in his spiritual journey, but most important was his own introspective mysticism. His final acceptance of Christianity was the culmination of a lifetime's search, traceable through his poetry back to his youth.

Lenten Illuminations

I

Not properly Catholic, some might say, to like it best
When no one's in the cool white church that few frequent
These sober-skied vocational afternoons in Lent.
There's sanctity in stillness, let it be confessed,
For one addicted much to meditationment—
One who has found this church a place full of replies
Given to what, wordless in him, asked that heart be learned
A Kempis lessons; toward the invisible, new eyes
In more than meditational consciousness be turned.

This afternoon it seemed unconvert self came in,
Puzzled to perceive one at the altar rails, unminding;
Could this be he—hereafter offered him to win,
And faith revealed wheretoward he pilgrim'd without finding?
O unforeknowing Ego, visitant in thought,
How were you thus the captive of that banished being?
Was it ordained—the long delayed deliverance brought—
The mercy that made plain your path? . . . O unforeseeing
Sad self, let's be together, now fortunate in freeing.

II

What were you up to—going into churches all those years
Of faith unfaithful? . . . Kneeling respectfully when others
   knelt,
But never a moment while reflective there alone.
The aids were manifest; but only for your eyes and ears,
In anthems, organ music, shaft-aspiring stone,
   And jewelled windows into which your mind might melt.
The sanctuary unseen was there; but not for you; not by the
   empty altar shown;
Not in the Crucifix. (Though each Good Friday you had felt
Almost unbearable the idea of how He died.)
From your default His face seemed ever turned aside.
Not then for you the arisen Word—not then the wrought
   remedial gift of tears.

How came it (ask your Angel—ask that vigilant voice)
That you this comfort found—that thus it grew to be—
This close, child-minded calm? . . . Look; those five candles lit
For five who have prayed your peace. (Candles were ever your
   choice
To tranquillize the mind, since boyhood.) They are what they are.
Two pennies for each. But Candlemas tells purity.
And we are told their innocent radiance will remit
Our errors. Although the lights of everlastingness, as someone
   said,
Can seem, for us poor souls, to dream so faint and far,
When at our broken orisons we kneel, unblest, unbenefited.

While you were in your purgatorial time, you used to say
That though Creation's God remained so lost, such aeons away,
Somehow He would reveal Himself to you—some day!
For Him, the Living God, your soul and flesh could only cry
   aloud.
In watches of the night, when world event with devildom went
   dark,
You implored illumination. But never being bowed

Obedient—never conceived an aureoled instance, an assuring
  spark.

Outcast and unprotected contours of the soul,
Why in these hallowed minsters could they find no home,
When nothing appeared more unpredictable than this—your
  whole
Influence, relief, resultancy received from Rome?
Look. Robed in white and blue, earth's best loved Lady stands;
Mother Immaculate; Name that shines to intercede.
Born on her birthday feast, until last year your hands
Kindled no candle, paid her heavenliness no heed.
Is it not well, that now you call yourself her child—
You and this rosary, at which—twelve months ago,—you might
  have shrugged and smiled?

This day twelve months ago—it was Ash Wednesday—one
Mid-way between us two toward urgent hope fulfilled
Strove with submission. Arduous—forbidding—then to meet
Inflexible Authority. When the work was willed,
The riven response from others to the task undone
Daunted a mind confused with ferment, incomplete:
There seemed so much renunciant consequence involved,
When independent questioning self should yield, indubitant and
  absolved.

III

This, then, brought our new making. Much emotional stress—
Call it conversion; but the word can't cover such good.
It was like being in love with ambient blessedness—
In love with life transformed—life breathed afresh, though yet
  half understood.
There had been many byways for the frustrate brain,
All leading to illusions lost and shrines forsaken. . . .
One road before us now—one guidance for our gain—
One morning light—whatever the world's weather—wherein
  wide-eyed to waken.

IV

This is the time of year when, even for the old,
Youngness comes knocking on the heart with undefined
Aches and announcements—blurred felicities foretold,
And (obvious utterance) wearying winter left behind.

I never felt it more than now, when out beyond these safening
  walls
Sculptured with Stations of the Cross, spring confident,
  unburdened, bold,
The first March blackbird overheard to forward vision
  flutes and calls.
You could have said this simple thing, old self, in any previous
  year.
But not to that one ritual flame—to that all-answering Heart
  abidant here.

Arbor Vitae

For grace in me divined
This metaphor I find:
A tree.
     How can that be?

This tree all winter through
Found no green work to do—
No life
     Therein ran rife.

But with an awoken year
What surge of sap is here—
What flood
     In branch and bud.

So grace in me can hide—
Be darkened and denied—
Then once again
     Vesture my every vein.

A Prayer in Old Age

Bring no expectance of a heaven unearned
No hunger for beatitude to be
Until the lesson of my life is learned
Through what Thou didst for me.

Bring no assurance of redeemed rest
No intimation of awarded grace
Only contrition, cleavingly confessed
To Thy forgiving face.

I ask one world of everlasting loss
In all I am, that other world to win.
My nothingness must kneel below Thy Cross.
There let new life begin.

~

EDITH SITWELL
(1887–1964)

The life of Edith Sitwell paralleled that of Siegfried Sassoon in several significant respects. Born within a year of each other, they spent a life of poetic probing of life's mysteries before finally resolving their quest in old age with their acceptance of Catholic Christianity. Sitwell was received into the Catholic Church in August 1955, writing of her conversion that it had given her 'a sense of happiness, safety and peace such as I have not had for years . . . What a fool I was not to have taken this step years ago.'

Still Falls the Rain
(The Raids, 1940. Night and Dawn)

Still falls the Rain—
Dark as the world of man, black as our loss—
Blind as the nineteen hundred and forty nails
Upon the Cross.

Still falls the Rain
With a sound like the pulse of the heart that is changed to the
    hammer-beat
In the Potter's Field, and the sound of the impious feet

On the Tomb:
    Still falls the Rain
In the Field of Blood where the small hopes breed and the
    human brain
Nurtures its greed, that worm with the brow of Cain.

Still falls the Rain
At the feet of the Starved Man hung upon the Cross.
Christ that each day, each night, nails there, have mercy on us—

On Dives and on Lazarus:
Under the Rain the sore and the gold are as one.

Still falls the Rain—
Still falls the Blood from the Starved Man's wounded Side:
He bears in His Heart all wounds,—those of the light that died,
The last faint spark
In the self-murdered heart, the wounds of the sad
    uncomprehending dark,
The wounds of the baited bear,—
The blind and weeping bear whom the keepers beat
On his helpless flesh . . . the tears of the hunted hare.

Still falls the Rain—
Then—O Ile leape up to my God: who pulles me doune—
See, see where Christ's blood streames in the firmament:
It flows from the Brow we nailed upon the tree
Deep to the dying, to the thirsting heart
That holds the fires of the world,—dark-smirched with pain
As Caesar's laurel crown.

Then sounds the voice of One who like the heart of man
Was once a child who among beasts has lain—
'Still do I love, still shed my innocent light, my Blood, for thee.'

~

T. S. ELIOT
(1888–1965)

T. S. Eliot is the most respected and revered poet of the twentieth cen-
tury—and the most popular according to the results of a nationwide
poll in the United Kingdom conducted by Waterstones in 1997. A
contemporary of Sassoon and Sitwell, his response to twentieth-century
materialism was akin to theirs, though his long poem The Waste Land
(1922) is regarded as the classic of literary modernism. In his criticism he
affirmed the importance of tradition, and he completed his poetic oeuvre
with his most profound work, Four Quartets *(1944). He became an*
Anglo-Catholic in 1927 and remained a devoted child of the Church
of England until his death in 1965.

From *The Rock*
From Chorus II

Of all that was done in the past, you eat the fruit, either rotten
    or ripe.
And the Church must be forever building, and always decaying,
    and always being restored.
For every ill deed in the past we suffer the consequence:
For sloth, for avarice, gluttony, neglect of the Word of God,
For pride, for lechery, treachery, for every act of sin.
And of all that was done that was good, you have the
    inheritance.
For good and ill deeds belong to a man alone, when he stands
    alone on the other side of death,
But here upon earth you have the reward of the good and ill
    that was done by those who have gone before you.
And all that is ill you may repair if you walk together in humble
    repentance, expiating the sins of your fathers;
And all that was good you must fight to keep with hearts as
    devoted as those of your fathers who fought to gain it.

The Church must be forever building, for it is forever decaying
    within and attacked from without;
For this is the law of life; and you must remember that while
    there is time of prosperity
The people will neglect the Temple, and in time of adversity
    they will decry it.

What life have you if you have not life together?
There is no life that is not in community,
And no community not lived in praise of God.
Even the anchorite who meditates alone,
For whom the days and nights repeat the praise of God,
Prays for the Church, the Body of Christ incarnate.
And now you live dispersed on ribbon roads,
And no man knows or cares who is his neighbour
Unless his neighbour makes too much disturbance,
But all dash to and fro in motor cars,
Familiar with the roads and settled nowhere.
Nor does the family even move about together,
But every son would have his motor cycle,
And daughters ride away on casual pillions.

Much to cast down, much to build, much to restore;
Let the work not delay, time and the arm not waste;
Let the clay be dug from the pit, let the saw cut the stone,
Let the fire not be quenched in the forge.

From Chorus VII

Men have left God not for other gods, they say, but for no god;
    and this has never happened before
That men both deny gods and worship gods, professing first
    Reason,
And then Money, and Power, and what they call Life, or Race,
    or Dialectic.
The Church disowned, the tower overthrown, the bells
    upturned, what have we to do
But stand with empty hands and palms turned upwards
In an age which advances progressively backwards?

From Chorus X

O Light Invisible, we praise Thee!
Too bright for mortal vision.
O Greater Light, we praise Thee for the less;
The eastern light our spires touch at morning,
The light that slants upon our western doors at evening,
The twilight over stagnant pools at batflight,
Moon light and star light, owl and moth light,
Glow-worm glowlight on a grassblade.
O Light Invisible, we worship Thee!

We thank Thee for the lights that we have kindled,
The light of altar and sanctuary;
Small lights of those who meditate at midnight
And lights directed through the coloured panes of windows
And light reflected from the polished stone,
The gilded carven wood, the coloured fresco.
Our gaze is submarine, our eyes look upward
And see the light that fractures through unquiet water.
We see the light but see not whence it comes.
O Light Invisible, we glorify Thee!

~

ROY CAMPBELL
(1901–1957)

Roy Campbell's poetry was greatly admired by his peers, particularly by T. S. Eliot and Edith Sitwell, but his satirical invective against the Bloomsbury Group and his vocal support for the Nationalists during the Spanish Civil War made him many enemies. He was received into the Catholic Church in 1935, whilst living in Spain, a country that he claimed had 'saved his soul'. 'To the Sun' and 'The Fight' depict the poet's conversion, whilst the sonnet 'San Juan de la Cruz' extols the praises of the great Spanish mystic whose poetry Campbell would later translate.

To the Sun

Oh let your shining orb grow dim,
Of Christ the mirror and the shield,
That I may gaze through you to Him,
See half the miracle revealed,
And in your seven hues behold
The Blue Man walking on the Sea;
The Green, beneath the summer tree,
Who called the children; then the Gold,
With palms; the Orange, flaring bold
With scourges; Purple in the garden
(As Greco saw): and then the Red
Torero (Him who took the toss
And rode the black horns of the cross—
But rose snow-silver from the dead!)

The Fight

One silver-white and one of scarlet hue,
Storm-hornets humming in the wind of death,
Two aeroplanes were fighting in the blue
Above our town; and if I held my breath,
It was because my youth was in the Red
While in the White an unknown pilot flew—
And that the White had risen overhead.

From time to time the crackle of a gun
Far into flawless ether faintly railed,
And now, mosquito-thin, into the Sun,
And now like mating dragonflies they sailed:
And, when like eagles near the earth they drove,

The Red, still losing what the White had won,
The harder for each lost advantage strove.

So lovely lay the land—the towers and trees
Taking the seaward counsel of the stream:
The city seemed, above the far-off seas,
The crest and turret of a Jacob's dream,
And those two gun-birds in their frantic spire

At death-grips for its ultimate regime—
Less to be whirled by anger than desire.

Till (Glory!) from his chrysalis of steel
The Red flung wide the fatal fans of fire:
I saw the long flames, ribboning, unreel,
And slow bitumen trawling from his pyre.
I knew the ecstasy, the fearful throes,
And the white phoenix from his scarlet sire,
As silver in the Solitude he rose.

The towers and trees were lifted hymns of praise,
The city was a prayer, the land a nun:
The noonday azure strumming all its rays

Sang that a famous battle had been won,
As signing his white Cross, the very Sun,
The Solar Christ and captain of my days
Zoomed to the zenith; and his will was done.

San Juan de la Cruz

When that brown bird, whose fusillading heart
Is triggered on a thorn the dark night through,
Has slain the only rival of his art
That burns, with flames for feathers, in the blue—
I think of him in whom those rivals met
To burn and sing, both bird and star, in one:
The planet slain, the nightingale would set
To leave a pyre of roses for the Sun.
His voice an iris through its rain of jewels—
Or are they tears, those embers of desire,
Whose molten brands each gust of song re-fuels?—
He crucifies his heart upon his lyre,
Phoenix of Song, whose deaths are his renewals,
With pollen for his cinders, bleeding fire!

R. S. THOMAS
(1913–2000)

R. S. Thomas is arguably the greatest poet in the English language since Eliot. Ordained into the Anglican ministry in 1937 he became vicar of the remote Welsh parish of Eglwysfach in 1954. His poetry resonates with a love for the Welsh landscape and people, and is tempered by a disdainful loathing of the encroachments of modern technology. Thomas's work derives its depth from his resilient yet troubled faith.

Hill Christmas

They came over the snow to the bread's
purer snow, fumbled it in their huge
hands, put their lips to it
like beasts, stared into the dark chalice
where the wine shone, felt it sharp
on their tongue, shivered as at a sin
remembered, and heard love cry
momentarily in their heart's manger.

They rose and went back to their poor
holdings, naked in the bleak light
of December. Their horizon contracted
to the one small, stone-riddled field
with its tree, where the weather was nailing
the appalled body that had asked to be born.

Praise

I praise you because
you are artist and scientist
in one. When I am somewhat
fearful of your power,
your ability to work miracles
with a set-square, I hear
you murmuring to yourself
in a notation Beethoven
dreamed of but never achieved.
You run off your scales of
rain water and sea water, play
the chords of the morning
and evening light, sculpture
with shadow, join together leaf
by leaf, when spring
comes, the stanzas of
an immense poem. You speak
all languages and none,
answering our most complex
prayers with the simplicity
of a flower, confronting
us, when we would domesticate you
to our uses, with the rioting
viruses under our lens.

~

DUNSTAN THOMPSON
(1918–1975)

Dunstan Thompson, an American poet who made his home in England, invites obvious comparisons with T. S. Eliot. In the 1940s he was lauded as one of the major poets of his generation and was compared favourably to contemporaries such as Dylan Thomas. His homosexuality, made manifest in much of his early poetry, made him hugely popular as a neo-decadent who was following in the dandified footprints of Oscar Wilde. Like Wilde, he converted to Catholic Christianity and renounced his homosexual lifestyle. From 1950 onwards his poetry is unabashedly Christian.

On the Lives of Some He Knew

They were so irremediably hurt, and straight from the start,
That Christ must see His Agony renewed in each shattered
    boy's heart,
And when in their improbable deaths they finally make contact
    with love,
Surely He will find not malice but sadness in the poor toys they
    made much of,
And give them a real childhood with Him, forever away from
    themselves:
—So, at least, it seems, watching them attempt to live, an
    unmastered art.

∼

Cardinal Manning

Prince, whom the people praised, though not the great
Men, milling with their money-boxes through
The palaces of chance and keeping state
From slums that opened out their hearts to you—
Your glory blazed through London when you died:
In gold and scarlet, you, ethereal, lay
Among the ragged ones, who were your pride,
As you were theirs, even more starved than they.
Your portrait shows you robed in God's own fire
Of love, a skeleton of charity,
Whose eyes, too brilliant for their time, inspire
One most unlike you momentarily
To share the sight you, hungry, could endure:
Christ crucified again in all His poor.

Walsingham

The pilgrims wandering in the curio shops
Gingerly touch Victorian artifacts—
The wrack of wash-stands mixed with servants' silver;
But buy their burnished postcards by the steps
That take them down and out before the sacked
Shrine and the long road that leads back to Calvary.

Some in hired cars, some in buses, some
Barefoot and burdened by outrageous crosses,
From which the eye, affrighted, turns to prize
A History of the Church in China; and in the shame
Of doing nothing to preserve the Masses
Said to save the soft-shod, perhaps one prays.

'Our Lady of the rapid transit, please
Winkle a servant from the prayer books printed
At prices to suit every purse, and from
The proud derision at the pious ways
In which the plastic rosary-beads are minted,
And to the wash-stand bring your servant home.'

From recollected cafés comes the murmur,
Like what five hundred years ago received
The palmer at the threshold, when the priests
At Compline sang: 'Salve Regina,' and armour
Clattered, as knights knelt and kings craved
Pity. For shrines, crowns, teapots, shatter—but prayer lasts.

From *Magdalen*

V

High in the noonday sky,
   His arms thrown open wide,
Love is about to die,
   With a thief on either side.

One He has welcomed home,
   The other prefers to hate,
Like the Pharisees, who roam
   In packs and wait and wait.

The soldiers there below,
   Bored and ashamed and blind,
Rattle the dice and throw
   Their lives away like rind.

The mocking scholars toss
   Their beautiful white heads
Far off; but at the Cross
   Who reads?

His mother, calm in pain,
   Adoring, and John,
The youngest friend, remain:
   Fair weather friendships gone.

And one other. She,
   Whose sins have had their share
In blossoming that tree,
   Offers her sorrow there.

Those tears are now for Him,
   Not for herself; she weeps
Outside her life; eyes swim
   Up from their own deeps.

His gift of sacrifice
   Opens her rusted heart:
With Him she pays the price
   Of love, that suffering art.

And so triumphant grief
   Makes her the fourth to stay:
Two innocents, a thief
   And a whore, together pray.

∽

GEORGE MACKAY BROWN
(1921–1996)

In many respects, George Mackay Brown and R. S. Thomas were kindred spirits. Both sought refuge from the artificiality of urban life in remote rural surroundings. In Brown's case this meant a life spent on his native Orkney, from which he rarely strayed. He was a convert to Catholicism and, as with Thomas, Christian faith infused depth into his observations of traditional rural life and the technology which threatened it.

Chapel between Cornfield and Shore

Above the ebb, that gray uprooted wall
Was arch and chancel, choir and sanctuary,
A solid round of stone and ritual.
Knox brought all down in his wild hogmanay.

The wave turns round. New ceremonies will thrust
From the thrawn acre where those good stones bleed
Like corn compelling sun and rain and dust
After the crucifixion of the seed.

Restore to that maimed rockpool, when the flood
Sounds all her luscent strings, its ocean dance;
And let the bronze bell nod and cry above
Ploughshare and creel; and sieged with hungry sins
A fisher priest offer our spindrift bread
For the hooked hands and harrowed heart of Love.

~

JOSEPH PEARCE
(1961–)

At the end of my garden of other men's flowers, outside
the gate, I have put this little wayside dandelion of my
own.

*These words were written by Field-Marshall Wavell to accompany the
inclusion of one of his own poems at the end of his ever-popular anthol-
ogy of verse,* Other Men's Flowers. *There is little I can do but point
apologetically at the precedent he set as I place one of my own efforts at
the conclusion of this volume. My only defence is that a verse depicting
the glory of sunrise seems appropriate as Christianity greets the dawn
of its third millennium.*

Summer Theologiae

Deep in the dark night of the soul
something stirs;
And bleary eyes,
depart from dream's dreary hole
as morning stars
in summer skies.
And ere sun rises
from sleep to slumber
and dawning of dawn,
alone one rises
in Lazarene lumber
to meet the morn.

And the world sleeps . . .

As gloaming fades
to stray and wander
in gladdening glades
to pray and ponder;
a voyeur visitor,
impertinent impostor,
inquisitive inquisitor,
mumbling *Pater Noster.*

In stillness to stare
at solitary hare
that accompanies the prayer.

Does it know?
Is it waiting?
Is it, as I,
anticipating?

It knows,
though what it knows,
it knows not:
distinctive
but instinctive,
and oblivious
of oblivion.
Subconscious friar
in Franciscan fraternity;
the hare's breath
is the hair's breadth
from here to eternity.

And the world sleeps . . .

And as the hare
grassward grazes,
without a care
for heavenward gazes,
something stirs . . .

Clouds clustered in pagan grey
turn a mythic, mystic rose,
Heaven's heralds of the day,
burning embers, amber glows.
Breeze through rushes,
shhhh . . . and hushes,
in silent awe at a maiden's blushes,
   Conceiving the Sun.
White, He rises
and soul surmises
resplendent disguises
   Concealing the One.

Corpus Christi!
Rising through the rose,
Sanguis Christi!
Skyward flows.

Heavenly Host
so new, so old,
as Holy Ghost
turns snow to gold.
Joy to Glory,
tinged with Sorrow,
endless story,
new tomorrow.

Thus transfixed
in transient transfiguration,
the impression
of mind's gaze
becomes expression
and finds praise.
From deep draught of thought
to prayer,
tasting sweet living water there,
divining Divinity.

But there are none so blind,
(blinded by the night),
as they who will not see,
they neither seek nor find,
(though reminded by the light),
They are but will not be.

Yet as life exhales,
passing the life sentence
through the Lamb's loam,
Love's exiles,
in repeated repentance,
long for Home.
And world's renunciation
wields annunciation,
divining Divinity;
as choirs of angels
dressed as birds
sing songs of praise
too blessed for words
in finite
infinity.

And the world sleeps . . .

~

Index of Authors

Index of Titles

Index of First Lines